SYSTEMS AND MEANING

Other titles in the
Systemic Thinking and Practice Series
edited by David Campbell & Ros Draper
published and distributed by Karnac Books

Credit Card orders, Tel: 020-7584-3303; Fax: 020-7823-7743;
Email: books@karnacbooks.com

SYSTEMS AND MEANING
Consulting in Organizations

Gitte Haslebo & Kit Sanne Nielsen

edited by
Gitte Haslebo

translated by
Dorte Herholdt Silver

Systemic Thinking and Practice Series
Work with Organizations

Series Editors
David Campbell & Ros Draper

London & New York
KARNAC BOOKS

First published in 2000 by
H. Karnac (Books) Ltd., 58 Gloucester Road, London SW7 4QY

A subsidiary of Other Press LLC, New York

British Library Cataloguing in Publication Data

A C.I.P. for this book is available from the British Library

ISBN 1 85575 235 2

10 9 8 7 6 5 4 3 2 1

Edited, designed, and produced by Communication Crafts

Printed in Great Britain by Polestar AUP Aberdeen Limited

www.karnacbooks.com

CONTENTS

v

ABOUT THE AUTHORS

GITTE HASLEBO was born in 1943, educated as a psychologist in 1970, and licensed by the Board of Psychology. She also has a Masters Degree from the United States and in further education in process consultation and systemic consultation, and a license in the Myers-Briggs Type Indicator.

Gitte has 15 years' experience in leader education, organizational development, and employee development training, and 5 years' managerial experience as manager of education at the Danish School of Public Administration and as personnel director at Kommunedata.

In 1991 Gitte founded her own consulting company in which she has worked extensively as a consultant in both public organizations and private companies. The tasks have concerned organizational development, team building, leadership development, consultant training, individual leader supervision, and career counselling.

KIT SANNE NIELSEN was born in 1953, educated as a psychologist in 1981, licensed by the Board of Psychology, and later authorized to practice clinical psychology. Since 1985 Kit has worked in organizational, leadership, and employee development, and in 1988 she established her own consulting company. Her continuing studies include one year of HD–organization, The Tavistock Centre's conferences (Leicester conferences), and systemic supervision and training at the Kensington Consultation Centre since 1991. She is also licensed in the Myers-Briggs Type Indicator and the California Psychological Inventory.

Kit has worked as a process consultant for both public organizations and private companies, and has developed and conducted leadership development training programs. As a consultant she has been involved with leader development, team building, problem solving, and the process of change within groups, departments, and organizations as well as individual leader counselling.

EDITORS' FOREWORD

A s the series editors, we have maintained a policy, with a few exceptions, of publishing first editions, so the series as a whole retains its reputation as a place where the reader can visit and be guaranteed fresh ideas and innovative practice, presented with conviction. This book by Haslebo and Nielsen was originally written in Danish and published in Denmark, where it has had four printings. We felt that these authors bring a new perspective to systemic work with organizations, and since there is far too little writing to match the amount of work being done in this area, we decided that this was an important book to add to our series. As a result, we worked alongside the authors in recasting their original volume to help it fit into the format of our series and to make it easily accessible to English-speaking readers.

Readers will immediately feel familiar with the values and the conceptual framework that underpin Haslebo's and Nielsen's work. They see organizational problems occurring in a particular context, they clearly trace the way problems arise out of relations amongst the different parts of the larger system, and they pursue the meanings that these problems have for individuals and organizations alike. Yet they also introduce new conceptual models, such as Kolb's notion of experiential learning.

But these authors are, above all, practitioners. They earn their living through their work with organizations, and it is this precious first-hand experience that must somehow be understood and articulated so that other practitioners can take the ideas into their own settings. The case studies are presented in some depth and are used to illustrate the way systemic concepts are translated into consultation work. The readers should also find that by considering that this work takes place in a different culture—in Denmark—there is a potential for comparison across cultures and institutions that adds an extra dimension to their own learning. Although this book is clearly written and accessible for practitioners starting out to work with organizations, it is the depth of experience of the authors that comes through on every page.

David Campbell
Ros Draper
London
June 2000

PREFACE

W ork as an organizational consultant can be challenging, unpredictable, stressful—and most gratifying. The stressful experiences include situations where we feel stuck and do not know in which direction to proceed. The gratifying experiences include situations where our clients discover a larger pattern of understanding which makes new solutions and actions possible, as well as situations where we as consultants succeed in creating for our clients better opportunities for dialogue and the exchange of ideas about and wishes for the future. Our background is that of many years of experience as psychologists and external consultants to private and public organizations. For the past ten years we have been greatly inspired by systemic thinking, which has helped us to look at our work with new eyes and to ask ourselves deeper and more humble questions: How do we know what we think we know? How do we manage to develop alternative hypotheses and discard those that do not work? How do we develop themes with which our client-system can connect? How do we create methods that encourage the participants to get involved and make their resources and competencies visible to each other?

In this book, we want to share our thoughts and experiences about fundamental questions like these with the reader. Along this line of thinking, we have the following intentions for the book.

First, we have sought to link theory with practice. We therefore draw from our own experiences in actual consultations. We are especially fascinated with the transition and linkage between thoughts and actions and between hypotheses and interventions, and this focus is one of the main axes of this book. We wish to avoid treating theory and practice separately. Instead, we try to capture the many subtle steps in the mind of the consultant from thought to action and from action to thought. This leads us to the next point.

The second axis for this book is the consultant's own thinking processes. We describe what we do as consultants as well as the process that led us to the choices that we made. What do we make of the events that take place in the interaction between the client-system and us as consultants? Through what filters do we view the events? How do we use the events as feedback and as a basis for developing new insights? How do we perceive the organizational problems when we, as consultants, attempt to predict future events? How can we listen "between the lines"? What can we as consultants learn from the events?

In order to elucidate these questions, we describe the events in the interaction with the client-system in two consultations as we perceived them, as well as the thoughts we had along the way. These thoughts are invisible to the client-system, but they are one of our tools. We are interested in discovering and defining what can move the thinking processes along, and what it takes to get out of situations where we feel that we have run out of ideas.

The third axis is the systemic perspective. Our paths towards working with psychological consultation in organizations have been different. Our common platform today is *systemic thinking*. We see the systemic approach as being excellently suited to bringing experiences and other psychological theories into play.

In addition, our conceptual baggage includes other theoretical frames of reference, such as the human resources school, general communication theory, organizational development, organizational culture, the learning organization, group dynamics, process consultation, psychodynamic thinking, psychoanalysis, and the psychological working environment. We consider this background important to our work as organizational consultants. But systemic thinking is what forms the overall framework and helps us to determine which perspective is the most promising in a given situation.

We do not intend to provide an independent presentation of systemic thinking—and certainly not a presentation of the various historical stages and schools in systemic thinking. Instead, we describe, in a very selective way, how we have applied systemic concepts in consultations.

The structure of the book is the following:

Chapter 1—"Organizational Consultation in a Systemic Perspective"—describes what is special about systemic consultation. Gitte Haslebo discusses how systemic thinking may provide inspiration for handling four key issues in organizational consultation: how to think about problems, how to define the system, how to understand change, and how to define the subject area.

In chapter 2—"Organizational Consultation and Learning"— Gitte Haslebo provides a view on individual and collective learning in organizations and then goes on to present her ideas on organizational consultation seen as the staging of collective learning processes.

This is followed by two case descriptions. Both describe two parallel tracks: on the one hand, the events and the consultant's experiences; on the other, the consultant's personal reflections, which serve as working hypotheses for the consultant.

In chapter 3—"Assess Our Manager and Expose His Shortcomings: A Consultation in a Private Company"—Kit Sanne Nielsen relates a consultation assignment that lasted seven months. The overall theme is "management and cooperation". The case study describes the difficulties that the manager and staff were experiencing and how the consultant, through various forms of intervention, was able to help the system to find new and more constructive approaches to management and cooperation. The consultant's own reflections during and after the process are presented as stages in a collective learning process. At the end of the chapter, the way systemic ideas were used to guide the work is illustrated.

In chapter 4—"'Free Us from the Past!': A Consultation in a Municipality"—Gitte Haslebo describes a consultation assignment that took place in a municipal department of social affairs and health. The client had requested help in coping with a past that was emotionally very burdensome concerning a manager who was no longer with the department. The case shows how a shift in focus from persons to organizational perspectives helped alter the understanding of the problem and how communication between different levels of the hierarchy was re-established. The chapter conclude with an account of the way that a number of systemic concepts were put into practice during the consultation.

In chapter 5—"Key Concepts in Systemic Thinking"—both authors discuss a number of key concepts: the linear and the circular form of understanding, from neutrality to irreverence, the professional domains, the formation of hypotheses, and intervention.

In chapter 6—"The Consultant's Cognitive Processes in Practice: When Two Consultants Work Together"—Kit Sanne Nielsen describes the challenges and opportunities inherent in working together with another consultant as part of a team or working together with an internal consultant in the organization that contains the client-system.

In chapter 7—"The Consultant's Cognitive Processes in Practice: Receiving Supervision"—Gitte Haslebo discusses situations and dilemmas where the consultant may benefit especially from supervision.

The style varies throughout the book; in the case studies we attempt to relate some interesting accounts from real life and connect them with systemic ideas, whereas the theoretical sections provide a more general introduction to some of the key concepts of systemic thinking. The chapters do not need to be read in the order that they appear. Some readers may prefer to read the case studies first, before proceeding to the general chapters, while others may prefer to read chapters 1, 2, and 5 before continuing with the case studies in chapters 3 and 4.

Our paths towards the systemic approach and, thus, our experience, thinking, and approaches are different. We have described our personal careers as organizational consultants in chapters 6 and 7. These two chapters, which also discuss various contexts for the consultant to work with her or his own learning processes, may appeal mostly to those consultants, managers, and students who are looking for inspiration for their own personal and professional development process.

We hope that by sharing our experiences with turning systemic concepts into practice we may inspire other consultants, managers, and employees to join in the common project that is about turning tacit knowledge into words and reasoning.

For a consultant, it is good to have a comprehensive toolkit. It is characteristic, however, of the consultant who works from a systemic perspective that the method has to materialize during the process in an interaction with the client-system, and that hypotheses and interventions have to be created on the spot. It is this creative process that we have attempted to capture.

Gitte Haslebo & Kit Sanne Nielsen

SYSTEMS AND MEANING

Organizational consultation in a systemic perspective

Gitte Haslebo

Systemic thinking is a new source of inspiration for the organizational consultant. In recent years, there has been a growing interest in Denmark in finding more holistic approaches to family therapy, counselling, supervision and organizational consultation.

Systemic thinking was first employed in individual and family therapy, and exciting methodological developments took place in several countries in the 1970s. The next obvious step was to use the approach in the supervision of those professionals who work with individual and family therapy.

One might expect it to be a small step to go from the supervision of professionals to consultation in organizations, but it has turned out to be a large and difficult one. Whereas the initial expectation was that concepts and methods from the field of therapy could be transferred directly to organizational consultation, it is now widely acknowledged that consultancy in larger systems necessitates additional considerations.

The organizational consultant has a pressing need for concepts that can be used to grasp the complexity of the larger system. Regardless of the issues at hand in the current consultation, the consultant needs to ask herself the following questions:

- How can I make myself useful to the entire organization?
- How can I grasp all those factors inside and outside the organization that have an impact on my handling of the assignment?
- How can I navigate the tension field between many different groups of stakeholders, all with their own points of view and wishes for the future?
- How can I maintain my curiosity and openness to the development potential at the same time as I am lectured about the organization's history, traditions, mental models, power struggles, and managers' and employees' perceptions of each other as enemies?

This book discusses how the organizational consultant can employ systemic thinking in practice to meet such challenges.

In the following, I will talk simply about systemic consultation instead of the more cumbersome term "organizational consultation in a systemic perspective".

How can systemic consultation be defined? It is not a well-defined form of consultation, but rather a loose assembly of ideas, concepts, and methods. One useful definition, however, can be offered:

> A consultant helps a client solve a problem through mutual exploration and understanding of the meaning which the inability to solve the problem has for the larger organization. The meaning shows in the way relationships are organized around the problem. [Campbell, Draper, & Huffington, 1991a]

This definition includes some of the concepts and understandings that characterize systemic thinking in particular. I am now going to paraphrase slightly the points that are made in the quote. One interesting idea is that what constitutes "the problem" is not the problem itself but the *meaning* that it represents to the organization. Another interesting point is that problems always have to do with—or affect—the human relations in the organization. A third point is that problem solving is considered a collaborative effort between the consultant and the client, where the client (and not the consultant) is the one to solve the problem.

When consultation is considered

Solving problems is an integral part of both managers' and employees' work. Sometimes the employees find it hard to do their work as well as they would like. There is friction in the cooperation, but they manage to overcome the problems and move on. In other instances, the problems grow so large that some members of the organization begin to consider drawing in a consultant. Let us take a closer look at how these events may occur in the organization.

When consultation is considered, it is always a case of one or more persons in the organization experiencing a problem, in the sense that there is a discrepancy between the desired state of affairs and the perceived state of affairs. Sometimes the focus is mostly on those aspects of the perceived state of affairs that one wants to get rid of or away from. The case described in chapter 3 deals with a request for help to avoid the confusion, uncertainty, and lack of self-esteem in the work situation that some members were experiencing due to the manager's problems with fulfilling his role as manager. The case in chapter 4 deals with a request for help to get over painful emotions stemming from events in the past.

In other cases the focus is more on the desired state of affairs. Some members of the organization have a vision of what the actual state of affairs should be.

Sometimes, the awareness of the problem has been under way a long time. In other cases it has occurred as the result of an internal crisis in the organization or in the relationship between the organization and its environment.

The recognition of the problem may occur close to the decision-makers in the organization or far away from them. If the organizational distance is small, the recognition may soon lead to the decision that the situation requires special attention. If the organizational distance is big, it may take months or years before any action is decided.

Initially, the considerations will be whether the problem can be solved with the use of internal resources. If this does not seem possible or appropriate, the next step is to find an external consultant. If the organization is already using a particular consultant, he or she will usually be asked for help in finding a good consultant. In my experience, three factors in particular influence the organization's choice of a consultant: personal knowledge of the consultant, the consultant's reputation in the organization's network, and knowledge of the consultant's qualifications and areas of expertise—often in that order.

The organization has limited knowledge of potential candidates and the extent to which their qualifications match the problem—especially if it is the first time a given problem occurs in the organization, and this is often the case when an external consultant is brought in.

It is therefore an ethical challenge for the consultant to always meet requests with an open and curious mind: "I wonder if consultancy is relevant in this case?" "I wonder what kind of consultancy?" "I wonder if I'm the right person?"

Any request—including requests that contain a clear and concise description of a specific solution (for example, we need personnel evaluation, structural changes, or cross-functional management training)—should lead to a preliminary phase where the problem and the connection between problem and solution are examined. This preliminary stage is described in more detail later in this chapter. For now, I simply want to point out that in the early stages it is important to leave open the question of whether consultation is a good idea at all and what sort of consultation is appropriate in the given case.

How to think about the problems

A problem exists when there is an unpleasant discrepancy between a perceived state of affairs and a desired one. A central idea within systemic thinking is that the existence of a problem requires an observer. The problem-owner is unable to reconcile the two conditions and in that sense is stuck with the problem. He feels that progress will be difficult or impossible. The actions that have been attempted so far have not had the desired effect, and the problem-owner cannot think of anything else to do.

When a member of an organization feels "stuck", the reason is often that the problem perception itself determines which events get noticed and how they are perceived. A vicious circle has been created, in the sense that one interprets other people's actions and statements in a way that fits the problem. To provide an example: a new employee perceives a problem—that the manager is not taking any interest in her. When the manager does contact her, she feels that he is watching her. This experience makes her feel that contacting management is dangerous, so she keeps this contact to a minimum. As a result, she spends less and less time with the boss, who has little possibility of finding her interesting. Thus, her understanding of the problem has contributed to maintaining the problem.

In other words, a problem is always a problem *to someone*. Problems do not arise independently of people but are created in our minds and in our interactions with each other. To the consultant it is important to investigate who finds the problem significant, who finds it insignificant, and who does not find it to be a problem at all. The consultant may also want to find out who was the first person to discover the problem, who was next, and so forth. How did the problem come to be defined the way that it did? At this point, it should be pointed out that problems are not considered more or less correctly defined, but they may be more or less "wisely" defined (see McCaughan & Palmer, 1994). To provide an example, a public organization had a problem that was defined as follows: "We get too many complaints. The number of complaints has to be reduced. Unfortunately, we are unable to do that, because we cannot hire any additional staff." An organization may live with this sort of problem definition for years, while frustration continues to mount. Whether or not the definition is "correct" is irrelevant. The key point is that it is "unwise", because all available energy is channelled into ideas about a particular change that is impossible, instead of the energy being invested in a creative analysis of the organization and the execution and quality of the work.

One explanation why organizations often create "unwise" problems is to be found in the complexity of events in an organization. Each manager and each employee, due to their position in the organization, has a particular vantage point from which they view the situation. It may be difficult to imagine or gain information about the views from other vantage points in the organization. Organizational position is one of the key factors in determining problem understanding.

It is a basic tenet of systemic thinking that problems—like other events or experiences—occur inside a frame of reference: a *context*. The concept of context arose within communication theory (Bateson, 1972) and has become a very common concept in the systemic literature. The use of it is an indispensable tool to the consultant who works from systemic inspiration. The concept comes from Greek and actually means "to weave together"; it is often interpreted as "the frame within which a phenomenon is understood".

Today, the concept is used in two ways, both in reference to the official definition of a situation and in reference to the unique meaning that people attribute to the situations that they are involved in. For example, a situation may be officially defined as an educational situation, and everybody knows this to be the context. This frame of reference, however, may include many different kinds of meaning: one person sees the situation as an evaluation by the consultant of the participants' management skills, another person sees it as management's way of helping the mid-level managers, while a third person sees it as an open forum for the exchange of experiences between colleagues. The first person views the activity as an *evaluation*, which is part of the relation between participants and consultant. The second person sees the same activity as a *help*, which is part of the relation between the participants and the management, and the third person sees it as an *exchange of experiences* between peers. Obviously, these three participants are going to notice very different things, based on the way that they experience the context. Similarly, their understanding of other people's actions and statements is going to be influenced by whether they see the context as evaluation, help, or the exchange of experiences and whether *the most visible relation* is the one between the participants and the consultant, between the participants and management, or between colleagues.

In this book, the word "context" is going to be used in the latter meaning—that is, as *the unique frame of reference within which events are understood*. As the previous example demonstrated, context has to do with both understanding and action. When we are unsure about the context, we become unsure about what is going on and how we can act. Communication becomes difficult, because we spend a considerable amount of energy on listening without really paying attention to what is being said, while wondering what it is that we—and the others—are engaged in. When we do not know what we are engaged in, we are unable to act. On the other hand, if the context of a given situation is clear, we can concentrate on the content of what is being said, and then we know how to act.

When events are labelled as problems, the challenge is to examine the frames of reference that make sense to the involved parties. These frames of reference are often implicit and, thus, not part of the shared pool of knowledge.

The context forms the invisible stage where the drama, "problem x", is acted out. If we move the spotlight from the problem to the stage, something new and different can happen. Once this has been done, there are many ways to solve a problem. For example, a problem may be solved when the conditions change in such a way that the symptoms (the large number of complaints, the poor working environment, the high level of absenteeism, and so forth) are interpreted within a new context. Or a problem is solved when the problem-owners realize how their own thoughts and actions are connected with the problem—because this may cause them to discover new possibilities of action.

In order for a problem to change, the consultant has to increase the total number of possibilities for dialogue and feedback. This may make it possible for the problem-owner to assume a *metaposition* to his problem. "Meta", originally a Greek word, means "above". In systemic thinking it is used to describe a situation where the person sees the problem from above (from a bird's eye-view) or from a different angle. When a problem is felt to be big or "impossible" to solve, the reason is often that the persons involved have trouble distancing themselves from the problem, which therefore seems overwhelming. In this situation, one can take a big step towards solving the problem by putting oneself in a meta-position in relation to the problem.

It is quite difficult for the person involved to assume a meta-position in relation to the problem. The consultant can help by asking questions such as: Who was the first to notice the problem? To whom is the problem worst? Who does not worry about the problem at all? What were things like before the problem arose? What would happen if the problem were to disappear?

The case study in chapter 4 describes several instances of this shift, for example at a point when the participants began to wonder how the problem had been allowed to exist for so long.

The consultant has to listen respectfully to the client's presentation of the problem and then challenge the client-system's problem definitions. Both case studies address the issue of how the consultant can handle this discourse about problems.

How to define the system

It is a common assumption that it is the organization, seen as a social system, that creates problems, and that the consultant therefore should want to know and understand as much as possible about the entire organization.

This is contrasted by the view that is characteristic of systemic thinking—that *it is the problem that defines the system* (Anderson, Goolishian, & Winderman, 1986). The consultant's work is based on the problem statements that she is presented with. Which persons and organizational entities are involved in these problem statements? The answer to this question may help the consultant to define the system that will be useful to include in a consultation. Defining the system is thus a *choice* to be made—and a choice that may have to be reconsidered during the course of a consultation.

In the process of finding the most appropriate definition, it may be useful for the consultant to consider which managers and employees are *parties in the consultation*. Often the consultant will meet the members of the organization in this order: first the referrer, then the commissioner, and finally the participants. The referrer is frequently called the contact person. He is the one who first contacts the consultant, either by telephone, letter, or personal contact. The commissioner is the manager or management team that has the formal authority over the resources (participants' time, the consultant's fee, use of conference-rooms, and so forth). The participants are those members of the organization who are going to be involved in the actual consultation. Some persons may have more than one role. The contact person may also be the commissioner, but that is rarely the case. In the case described in chapter 4, nobody had more than one role. In some cases, the contact person and the commissioner will also be included as participants. Whether or not this is appropriate is one of the important issues to be resolved in the initial stage.

In Figure 1.1, relations that are characterized by direct contact with the consultant are shown with full-drawn lines, while relations characterized by indirect contact are shown with dotted lines. Thus, the consultant may be able to observe directly what goes on between herself and the contact person but be unable to

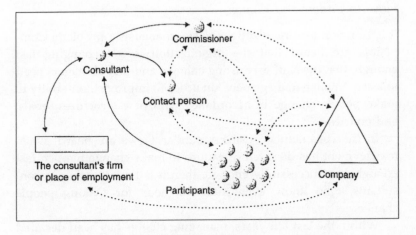

FIGURE **1.1.   Parties and relations in consultation**

observe what happens in the relation between the commissioner and the participants.

Figure 1.1 also includes "the company" in order to illustrate that there may be agents elsewhere in the company whom the consultant does not meet, but who influence the consultation. The consultation includes the consultant and her firm or place of employment.

It is important for the systemic consultant to consider what characterizes all these relations. For example: How is the contact person viewed in the company? What made this particular person the contact person? What is the nature of the relation between the contact person and the commissioner—do they consider themselves in cooperation or competition? What does the rest of the company expect of the consultant—perhaps based on previous experiences with other consultants? What does the consultant's place of employment expect of, for example, the consultant's choice of methods, and what do the consultant's colleagues consider success criteria? And so forth. The point here is that the various *understandings of the problem and the possibilities for solving it are embedded in all these relations.* Exactly how, the consultant will not know from the beginning: in order to make progress, it is important that she explore the relations.

How to understand change

It is common for organizations to see change as a problem. Complaints are heard that the organization is not changing fast enough, that the staff is resisting change, and that managers need to learn "change management" in order to improve their ability to make people change in accordance with new structures, goals, and policies.

In the consultancy business, similar views are heard: when management has declared its failure to make change happen fast enough and successfully enough, then it is time to bring in consultants, who know even more methods for making people change.

Within the last ten years, managing change has been declared one of the greatest management challenges.

Systemic thinking offers a radically different view of the dynamics of change. Here, the basic idea is that organizations as well as people in organizations are constantly undergoing change. Change is not the problem. But the meaning or interpretation that the members of the organization attribute to the changes may be experienced as a problem. When employees declare, for example, the latest reorganization to be a problem, the reason may be that they see top management's decision to restructure as a disparagement of their efforts until then. This is not stated openly; instead, the structure comes under fire.

An organization may be seen as a complex network of relations between people, their ideas, mental models, values, attitudes, and dreams for the future. Since these relations are valuable to people, human development requires a reasonable degree of agree-ment between change and the relations that the individual is a part of. It is an important point in systemic thinking that change is seen as being determined by the structure of the system. Outside "disturbances" may occur, but it is the system that decides how it is going to respond to these influences (Maturana & Varela, 1980).

In this sense, change is determined from the inside—to a greater extent than being controllable from the outside. This, in effect, is a controversial idea: that managers, consultants, parents, and so forth are unable to make other people change as a result of direct outside influences. This can be an extremely disturbing idea to goal-directed and impatient managers and consultants who are measured by themselves and others on their ability to produce quick, visible results.

This widespread view of success also includes an understanding of change as a linear process, where each of the stages depends on the outcome of the previous stage and provides input for the following stage. Change management is seen as a rational process that the manager can think out, plan, and force the staff through, thus achieving the desired outcome. The weak link in this view is the idea that human thoughts and meaning-forming processes can be controlled from the outside. Even the most gifted and communicative manager (or consultant) is unable to imagine the multiplicity of interpretations that employees create individually and in interaction with each other.

To the systemic consultant, the task is not to help management control the change or to change people directly. Nevertheless, it is an essential part of the systemic consultant's expertise to be able to work with processes of change. The purpose for the consultant is to find new ways of creating new contexts, where new ideas can arise, where people want to claim the ownership of new ideas, and where they have the possibility of incorporating them into existing relations.

When the frustrations in an organization are particularly strong and attached to one or more fundamental changes, such as a merger or a reorganization, we often find that both management and staff have a tremendous need for making sense of what appears as madness. At the same time, however, the possibilities for an open dialogue are very slim. The time spent together is limited, and it is often felt to be dangerous to express questions and concerns about the changes. As a result, many people feel alienated from the changes, which then remain a foreign body in the organization.

How to define the subject area

Throughout the consultancy business, the subject area is defined very differently. In traditional consultancy tasks, the focus is either on the changes in structure, technology, and systems or on the development of the members of the organization. In the first case, the thinking behind the consultation is as follows: first, an investigation will be carried out to analyse the problems, identify the causes, and find the best solution. Once the solution is found and described, it is to be communicated throughout the organization. Then comes the implementation phase, during which the employees are trained, their acceptance is secured, and a number of old procedures are to be abandoned and replaced by new ones.

Often this implementation process does not run as smoothly as expected. Some employees may not want to learn new procedures; some managers may not want to implement the new procedures; some managers and employees may encounter unanticipated difficulties; and so forth. This is when "the human factor" becomes a problem. The solution was good, but managers and staff "resist change"—as people say. What went wrong was that the individual managers and employees did not get the time and opportunity or the assistance to attribute meaning and value to the new solutions together with others.

In the second case, the focus is on the development of the members of the organization. Many manager education programmes and employee training activities belong in this category. The individual is temporarily removed—often physically as well—from the organization and given the opportunity to work with his personal development (for example, a course in assertion training) or to gain new knowledge (for example, a course in human resources management). The rationale behind these activities is, first of all, that the individual will get renewed energy from being given a chance to learn and grow, and, secondly, that the person is going to be able to apply his new knowledge, insight, and skills on the job. Often both aspects are realized as planned, but sometimes the second point turns out not to be that simple: the new knowledge is not put into use in the company. The reason for this is that learning and developing in an educational context tend to be "abstract", in the sense that they are not directly linked to the person's real life on the job. The individual has to create these connections through reflections after the event.

To the systemic consultant, the subject area is neither the structure per se, nor the technology per se, nor the individual per se, but the *individual in the organizational context*.

Consequently, it is of great interest to the consultant to explore how the individual member of the organization is connected to his or her role.

When a person gets a job in a public or a private company, he is allotted a role that includes a specific position in the organization chart and a set of tasks to be carried out. This is a contractual relationship that includes both a formal and a psychological contract. The formal contract is described in the employment contract and in the terms of the collective agreement. The term "psychological contract" refers to the explicit—or, frequently, implicit—mutual expectations. The person is expected to contribute in certain ways to the company's current activities and future development, and the company is expected to provide pay, ongoing training, a satisfactory and empowering working environment, and so forth. The degree of formalization in terms of organization charts, job descriptions, policies, guidelines, and so forth varies, depending on the type of organization and organizational culture. But all organizations have some level of formalization. Typically, the degree of formalization will be in an inverse relationship to the degrees of freedom experienced by the individual. To some extent, the organizational culture can modify this relationship: the formalization exists, but it is not taken seriously. The explicitness of the hierarchy and the impact of the formalization are important issues for the consultant to explore.

To the systemic consultant, then, it is important to be curious about the individual's own assessment and view of his role, tasks, and relations to management and colleagues. How does the person perceive the opportunities and constraints offered by the role, and what does the membership of the organization mean to the individual? It is my experience from many consultations that the mutual expectations to roles and relationships are usually implicit and—when they are made explicit—turn out to be poorly matched. There have also been situations, however, where an individual was afraid to express his thoughts, for fear that expectations would turn out to be conflicting, but where this turned out, in the ensuing process, *not* to be the case, much to his surprise and relief.

Organizational cultures vary a great deal in terms of their norms for openness. In some organizational cultures, thoughts and ideas concerning roles and relations are "off limits". Not that this is ever stated directly, but it is in the air that such considerations are a personal issue that has no room in the public life of the organization. Therefore, the expression of thoughts, considerations, and concerns is only allowed outside the organization or in the informal networks within the organization, where other rules apply. In organizational cultures of this type the formal aspects are predominant, and it is difficult for the individual to find legitimate ways of connecting the formal and personal aspects of organizational life.

In other organizational cultures—for example, in great parts of the social and educational areas—openness is commonly held to be a sign of a good working environment and good relations. The greater the openness—also concerning family life and recreational activities—the better. In this setting, frustrations often arise if conversations in the workplace do not live up to this ideal. The consultant then meets a strong request to make something happen "so that we can become completely open to one another". These organizational cultures often lack concepts for the formal aspects of organizational life. The members of the organization view each other as private individuals who also carry out a job together. If difficulties do arise, they are often understood to be the result of likes and dislikes that cannot be altered. Problems and conflicts, therefore, are very difficult to handle.

In the former type of organizational culture, the personal aspects disappear or are made illegitimate. In the latter type, the person, to some extent, stands "naked", without the protection offered by the role.

This line of thinking, which has *the individual person in the organizational context* as its subject area, also implies that the methods of the systemic consultant have to respect the hierarchy, the formal power structures, and the persons with managerial authority. The commissioner has to be able to rely on being accorded this respect, but respect alone is not enough. It has to be combined with both support and challenge, in the sense of a curiosity towards the thoughts, mental models, and suggested solutions that are embedded in the management system. Without this curiosity, the consultant runs the risk of becoming subordinate to the management as a sort of stand-in manager, which does not add anything new to the organization. In that case, the consultant has lost her intellectual freedom of movement.

CHAPTER TWO

Organizational consultation and learning

Gitte Haslebo

Consultation in organizations can be viewed as a special framework for problem solving. Problem solving requires learning. In this chapter I therefore focus on how individual and collective learning take place in organizations and how organizational consultation can be viewed as the staging of collective learning processes.

Learning in organizations

Let me make it clear from the beginning: learning is a psychological process. *People* learn, *organizations* do not. The strong current interest in "the learning organization" and in "organizational learning" reflects a great need to be able to handle frequent and unpredictable changes in our environment. Much of the literature, however, is full of vague concepts that may give the reader the faulty impression that organizations are capable of learning (for example, Dixon, 1994, and Pearn, Roderick, & Mulrooney, 1995). Both concepts suggest that the organization is an agent. This is misleading, and I will therefore in the following refrain from using these concepts at all, and instead draw inspiration from the many exciting ideas that are also present in this literature.

These ideas concern the questions of how the individual member of the organization succeeds in learning something that can be used in action, how new understanding is developed and shared by many members of the organization, and how individual and collective learning processes are connected.

In the literature, individual and collective learning are usually treated as two separate phenomena. One reason why Nancy Dixon's work is so fascinating is that she tries to elucidate how the two are connected in the organization. Her discussion is based on a constructionist view of learning. In this systemic view, learning is seen as the act of interpreting experience. How the individual interprets experience and tries to make sense of it is unique to each person, and the meaning that is created mediates actions. To develop this view of learning, she draws on experiential learning theory, which offers a holistic perspective on learning, focusing on the integration of experience, perception, cognition, and behaviour. Some of the valuable sources to the experiential learning theory stem from the philosopher John Dewey, the founder of American social psychology Kurt Lewin, and the developmental psychologist Jean Piaget (see Dewey, 1934; Lewin, 1951; Piaget, 1971).

The historical development in this tradition is brilliantly described by David A. Kolb in his book *Experiential Learning: Experience as the Source of Learning and Development*, which has been a stepping-stone for many writers and consultants, who have subsequently sought to understand learning in organizational contexts (Kolb, 1984).

Kolb defines learning as "the process whereby knowledge is created through the transformation of experience" (Kolb, 1984, p. 38). How this takes place Kolb describes in his model for the individual learning cycle. The learning process has two dimensions—prehension and transformation—which represent opposite orientations.

"Prehension" refers to the two distinct ways of grasping or taking in experience in the world. Prehension can take place in

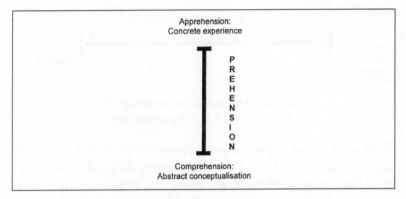

FIGURE 2.1.   The individual learning cycle:
the dimension of prehension

two different ways: we can either grasp our experience by relying
on the tangible, felt qualities of immediate experience, or we can
grasp our experience by relying on conceptual representation (see
Figure 2.1).

The first way is called "apprehension", and the second "comprehension". We can apprehend a cold draft or a red colour in a
given situation. Apprehension is an instantaneous registration of
experience. We just know. On the other, hand, comprehension of
experience is slower. We search for words and concepts and may
conclude, for example, that a given situation involving a large
number of employees constituted a "conflict-ridden meeting". The
two different ways of grasping experience have interesting implications for communication. It is difficult to communicate our
concrete experiences to each other, whereas concepts can be communicated through language.

Prehension alone, however, is not sufficient for learning to take
place. What is grasped has to be transformed into knowledge,
which can take place in one of two ways—either through internal
reflection or through actions in the external world (see Figure 2.2).
Kolb considers the two dimensions, prehension and transformation, as equally important to learning.

It is one of Kolb's points that the more the possibilities for
learning increase, the easier it is to move all the way around in the
learning cycle. People are different, however, because they have

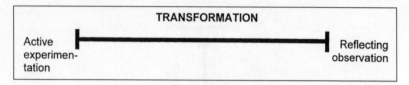

FIGURE 2.2. The individual learning cycle:
the dimension of transformation

developed different preferences concerning how to function. In his book, Kolb describes different learning styles, their development and consequences. Kolb makes the point that individual learning, of course, is not an isolated process, but one that takes place in interaction with other people. His main interest is to look at learning in relation to child development, education, and adult learning.

Kolb describes the individual learning processes as circular. I prefer to talk about learning loops, as learning is a progressing movement where you never return to your point of departure (see Figure 2.3).

This is the point where organizational psychologists take over. They do this by bringing the discussion into the organizational context and by asking what structural and cultural factors in the

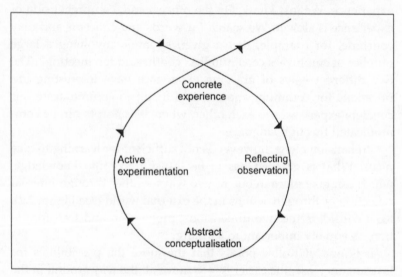

FIGURE 2.3. The individual learning loop

organization are capable of promoting learning in the individual employees and inviting them to share new knowledge (Swieringa & Wierdsma, 1992).

A fascinating answer to this question is offered in the book *The Organizational Learning Cycle: How We Can Learn Collectively* (Dixon, 1994). Dixon attempts to link the individual learning cycle with a collective learning cycle and in this connection talks about an organizational learning cycle.

Again I prefer the picture of the loop instead of the closed circle. Figure 2.4 illustrates how the individual learning loop can be combined with the organizational learning loop.

In order to avoid the misleading concept I mentioned earlier— that organizations learn—I will talk instead about those organizational activities that may promote collective learning processes. By "collective learning processes" I mean *individual learning in many members of the organization who interact with each other, and where the individual learning leads to new shared knowledge in the organization.*

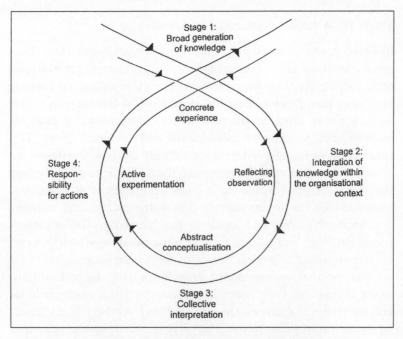

FIGURE 2.4.   The organizational learning loop combined with the individual learning loop

In the following, I take my point of departure in Dixon's model and expand it with my own experiences with various types of organizations.

Stages in the collective learning process

Collective learning processes require there to be people in the organization—preferably many people—who get the opportunity to participate in activities that go through all four stages (see Figure 2.4). The larger the company is, and the more it is divided into specialized organizational units, the more likely it is that distinct organizational units deal with each stage separately. This severs the connection between the stages, and the possibility for collective learning is lost.

Stage 1: *A broad generation of knowledge*

In Stage 1, there is a *broad generation of thoughts and ideas*. This generation may take place outside the organization, for example by gathering opinions from customers or other interested parties, or it may take place among the employees of the company. The focus is not so much on the production of fragmented data as on contributions to coherent perceptions and understandings. The production of fragmented data would only increase the degree of detail, without necessarily increasing the dynamic complexity (see chapter 4). A prerequisite for a *broad* generation is an openness, both between the organization and its surroundings and between organizational units and levels in the hierarchy. The organizational structure and culture influence the extent to which this can be accomplished as well as the terms for the exchange.

The external generation of knowledge will depend, among other things, on how introvert or extrovert the organizational culture is. Some cultures are introvert and not very likely to actively invite outside views. Maybe it is mostly complaints that are able to get through and attract attention. Other organizational cultures, on the other hand, are more extrovert and reward the import of interesting and unusual views to the company. Read more about this in the book by Bridges, who has developed an insightful typology for organizational cultures based on Jung's work (Bridges, 1992).

In very bureaucratic organizations, information is generated primarily within the individual organizational units. The production department, the sales department, and the economy department each produce their own data. These data are seen primarily as the department's own tools and are therefore primarily produced to match the department's own needs.

The generation of information provides the material that management and staff have to work with in the following stages. A broad and systematic dissemination of information and points of view is a first step. This is not a matter of quantity alone, in the sense of "the more the better". More may actually be worse. For example, the extensive production of detailed data in a department may make it more difficult to get the big picture. A wide generation across the board is more important than quantity, because it makes it easier to sort through the data and focus on the essential aspects.

The activities in Stage 1 aim to expand the area, using *the available meaning structures* in the organization. This concept comes from Dixon (1994).

She explains how meaning structures in an organization can be private, collective, or accessible. The *private meaning structures* are the thoughts and views that the individual member of the organization chooses to keep to himself. His reasons for doing so may be many and numerous: He may consider it risky to express a particular view, or see it as a personal advantage to keep his opinions to himself. In these cases, the private meaning structure is explicit and articulated. Private meaning structures, however, may also be implicit, in the sense that the person has not yet put them into words, but nevertheless acts on the basis of them.

Meaning structures in organizations can also be collective—that is, they are shared by many members of the organization. *Collective meaning structures* may deal with success criteria for the work that is carried out, ideas about customers, standards for communication, goals and strategies, and so forth. Again, collective meaning structures may be explicit or implicit. The *explicit* ones, for example, may be the official image that top management presents to the outside world, or they may be the shared understanding that "we are a progressive municipality" or "we are a company in the midst of a crisis". The *implicit* ones are made up of all the assumptions that are taken for granted and therefore do not come up for discussion. The concept of "implicit meaning structures" is related to the everyday concept of "intuition". When acting intuitively, we act without pausing. We just "know" that this is the way to do *this*. It is good to be able to act intuitively: it is fast, it feels right, and it often produces the desired results. Similarly, there are benefits to the implicit meaning structures: the organization saves time, work is done quickly, and re-assessments are unnecessary. On the downside, it is difficult to get to test the validity of an implicit meaning structure and change it. In order, for example, to test the validity of the assumption that a given manager is "dangerous", it is necessary both to put it into words and to find data to assess it by.

Various organizational activities aim to develop implicit collective meaning structures. This is the case, for example, with the initiation courses for new employees and the joint activities that are to promote the "team spirit" in the company. The unintentional and indirect learning that takes place through structures and processes is a theme that has held my interest for many years (Haslebo, 1973).

In some organizational cultures, the collective meaning structures are very prominent. This is often the case in old companies, rich in tradition, which emphasize the socialization of newcomers in order to secure the proper company spirit. In other organizations the collective meaning structures are less prominent, and "team spirit" may be attributed less importance.

The third category of meaning structures in organizations is referred to as *accessible meaning structures*, because these structures can be made the object of common exploration within the organization. The greater the latitude for communication and the formation of meaning, the greater the chances for collective learning.

Stage 2:   *The integration of knowledge*
within the organizational context

In Stage 2 there is an *integration of new knowledge within the organizational context*. This integration has both a physical and a cognitive aspect. The new knowledge has to be transferable in order to become available to a large number of people in the organization, and the information must be cognitively accessible.

The division into organizational units and hierarchical levels often makes it difficult to transfer knowledge. Several factors play a part in this. If an employee or a manager spends most of her time in her own department or on her own level, the practical opportunities for exchanging knowledge across the divisions are going to be limited. In addition, each department selects the information that seems most comprehensible and useful. Thus, each department may wind up holding its own pieces of information, which the members know in depth but with no ability to see how the pieces fit into the bigger picture.

Of necessity, there is a high degree of selection and filtering. When management and staff members complain that "nobody ever tells us anything", it is rarely because they get *too little* information, but because they lack relevant information for carrying out their jobs.

Transferring knowledge up and down through the organizational hierarchy can be problematic too. In organizational cultures where it is considered a sign of weakness to admit that there is a problem, information about potential problems is often kept to a minimum, and the message conveyed to the higher levels is "We're doing fine". In my work as a consultant I have often found that top management had a far more positive impression of how the organization was doing than people further down in the hierarchy.

Transferring knowledge is a first step, but does not necessarily lead to cognitive integration. In some organizational cultures, knowing *who* was involved in the production of the new knowledge is just as important as the actual content of the knowledge. This is typical of organizations with a *power culture*. Here, the power figure's acceptance of managers and employees in effect determines how much clout they will have. Similarly, knowledge produced by external consultants is often met with scepticism. There is a common understanding (implicit or explicit) of who the key persons in the company are. These people are recycled endlessly in all important committees. Everybody in the organization knows that it is more important to ensure the participation of these key persons than to make up project groups based on knowledge and qualifications.

On the other hand, members in organizations with a *role-based culture* will be sceptical of knowledge produced in other organizational entities than their own, but very open to knowledge produced in cooperation with outside experts. The reason is that members of role-based cultures tend to hold expertise in very high esteem. See Handy (1986) and Swieringa and Wierdsma (1992) for a more detailed description of these organizational cultures.

Stage 3: *Collective interpretation*

In Stage 3, a collective interpretation of the new information, points of view, and thoughts takes place. It is important to be aware that receiving information and gaining meaning from it are two different things.

The interpretation of information is influenced by the recipient's organizational position. Every day in organizations, numerous individual interpretations are carried out. The managing director interprets the events at a management meeting from his perspective, the mid-level manager from a mid-level perspective, and the employee, who later reads the minutes of the meeting, interprets events on the basis of his particular background, experiences and expectations. Interpretations also take place at group-level. "We sales people feel . . .", "We nurses must demand . . ." or "We in the home care division will no longer put up with . . .". The individual member of the organization always belongs to an organizational unit or a professional group, and many interpretations are based on the group's point of view. The perspective is not always stated as explicitly as in the examples above. Interpretations often appear as a truth or a conclusion to the individual, simply because he or she is not aware of any other interpretations. Only rarely do the sales people, nurses, or home carers learn how the world might appear from other vantage points.

The big challenge in relation to collective learning, then, is to take the step from individual or group-based interpretations to collective interpretations. In order for this to happen, the members need practical opportunities of getting together with managers and colleagues who have other organizational perspectives. The size, structure, organization of the work, meeting structure, and planning of additional training are all factors that can promote or inhibit this possibility. Companies with a task-based culture often use temporary project groups made up of employees from different departments in varying combinations. In this case, one is very likely to hear about and take in other perspectives. Some public and private companies have experimented with job rotation schemes and staff policy initiatives in order to promote the mobility between groups and departments within the company. Such initiatives also increase the members' ability to incorporate different perspectives into their interpretations.

The extent to which the organizational culture is based on egalitarian values is also of importance. Dixon defines the three most important values as the freedom to express oneself without fear of retribution, equality, and mutual respect (Dixon, 1994). Power relations, status differences, and informal success criteria are some of the factors that can undermine these values. In the power culture, favouritism will reduce the notion of equality and mutual respect and, thus, the personal courage to express opinions and interpretations. In the role-based culture hierarchical status differences influence the assessment of opinions, and in the task-based culture it may be informal success criteria, such as access to the mass media, that reduce the sense of equality.

It is an important task for the consultant to promote activities and skills for carrying out open dialogues where points of view can be expressed, listened to, explored, and challenged. The importance of dialogue in promoting the collective interpretation lies both in the possibility of discovering what we ourselves actually think—that is, an exploration of the private, implicit meaning structures—and in the possibility of leaving the egocentric perspective behind by discovering the multiplicity of understandings. One might also say that *dialogue is the workout that makes the mind agile.*

Stage 4: *Assuming responsibility for actions*

In Stage 4 in the collective learning process, one *assumes responsibility for actions* on the basis of the interpreted meaning. Here, it makes a difference how clearly the formal decision-making authority in the organization is defined, and how easy (or how difficult) the organizational culture makes it for management and employees to make decisions and to assume responsibility both for decisions and actions.

In organizations with a role-based culture the formal decision-making authority is often clearly defined through job descriptions. However, there is often a very punishing attitude towards mistakes, which makes it risky to openly assume responsibility. Unclear decisions are seen as an advantage, because the obscurity makes it easier to make excuses later, should the need arise.

In organizations that have a task-based culture with a complex matrix organization and widespread delegation of authority it may be unclear, both to management and employees, how certain types of decisions are to be made.

As a consultant I have also met companies where decision-making and action were valued so highly that the weak point was in making sure that everything was based on the collectively interpreted meaning. There may have been data gathering and discussions in an earlier stage, but at some point the project is pressed for time, and actions are taken that do not build on the previous stages. The outcome of this is often more of the same. Everything remains the way it was—with great frustration as the result. Managers and employees will ask, "What was the point, then, with all those surveys and discussions?"—And if a similar approach is suggested later, they are less likely to participate actively.

Consultation as the staging
of collective learning processes

There are many approaches to understanding systemic consultation. One of them is to see the consultant's work on the overall
design, contract, planning, and realization of activities as the creation of structures and processes that improve the conditions for
collective learning processes. In accordance with the previous description of change and learning, the consultant cannot guarantee
that collective learning will take place. But the systemic consultant
will attempt to use her expertise and creativity to create additional possibilities for collective learning that are different from
those that the organization itself is able to provide.

Where Dixon's considerations ended with a description of the
impact of various organizational factors on the collective learning
process, I will take things one step further and describe how this
model may be made applicable to the systemic consultant's considerations and concrete work. (See also chapter 3.)

What, then, are the key issues in the design and execution of a
consultation, seen in relation to collective learning? This question
will be the topic of the following sections.

Defining the participant group

In the initial stages of a consultation, which and how many of
the organization's managers and employees should be included
as participants is often a major and open question. Neither the
referrer nor the commissioner necessarily has a very clear or useful idea about this. As mentioned in chapter 1, the point of departure of any consultation is a perceived problem. In consequence,
the makeup of the participant group must also be based on considerations concerning the relations that various managers and
employees have to the problem. As systemic literature often
points out, it is more important to consider how the problem defines the system—than how the system defines the problem
(Anderson, Goolishian, & Winderman, 1986).

In this connection, the following questions come up: Whose
problem is it—that is, who perceives it as a problem? Who has

information about the problem? Who wants to, or is willing to, contribute to the consultation? Who has the decision-making authority in relation to the problem? In an actual consultation, the various questions do not usually point to the same group of people. Some people who have information about the problem may not want to participate, for example because they think that other problems are more urgent. Others may be keen to contribute information but lack the relevant decision-making authority. The two case studies illustrate the potential complexity of the situation (see chapters 3 and 4).

The commissioner may often want to include as few people for as short a time as possible. A consultation is costly to the company, which has to pay managers and staff while they participate. This means both expensive salaries and the delay of activities related to clients and customers that might otherwise have taken place. The commissioner will therefore be in a situation where long-term benefits have to be weighed against short-term costs.

From the consultant's point of view, there is often great uncertainty about what will be the most useful selection of participants. At the same time, this is a decision that has to be made during the initial contract stage. As the consultant will typically be very concerned about the potential negative consequences of leaving key persons out, she will often tend to want to include as *many* people as possible—and often for a longer period of time than the commissioner had in mind.

Naturally, the consultant has to respect the company's economic possibilities and priorities. This means that the consultant has to consider how small the group can be, *without compromising the possibilities of going through the collective learning process*. It is the consultant's responsibility to make the necessary assessments of this question and to include it in the contract negotiations. In most cases, it is possible to reach a common ground that both the commissioner and the consultant can get behind.

In some cases, in my work as a consultant, I have found this common ground hard to reach. I will mention one example: in an organization, the commissioner (the managing director) perceived a big problem in the form of a conflict between two departments, and he wanted an investigation into the causes of this conflict. The commissioner's first suggestion was for the managers of the two departments to be involved; he did not want to participate himself. The managers of the two departments, however, did not see the conflict between the two of them as the most serious problem. Instead they felt that other problems were more pressing, such as poor communication from the top down. In such a case, it becomes a key issue whether the managing director is willing to enter into a dialogue with the nearest lower levels. If not, there is a great risk that the managers will have little motivation to express their views or make use of other people's views. It is also difficult to imagine how any new insight could be turned into decisions and action.

The time factor

Problem solving and learning take time. The time factor involved in the occurrence, recognition, maintenance, and solving of problems is crucial. It is therefore important to look into the history of the problem. How long do various members of the organization feel that the problem has existed? When did they first notice signs of its existence? How long was it from the first signs until it was decided to conduct a consultation? All things being equal, it is true that *the longer a problem has been "underway", the longer it is going to take to solve it*. This includes not just the time spent in sessions with the consultant and the participants, but also—and perhaps especially—the duration of the entire consultation process and the scheduling of the time spent in sessions.

Consultation means setting off and reserving time for learning, but there is a limit as to how fast that learning can happen. Sometimes the participants express this explicitly: "I can't stomach any more right now, I need a break", "That really is food for thought—I need some time to think about that", "We need time for it to sink in", "I am going to test that idea in the next meeting" or "That was unexpected, I need time to digest it." Interestingly enough, many of these metaphors stem from the area of biology. Learning, too, has a biological basis. The processes in the individual and collective learning processes take their time. It takes time to recreate the history of the problem. It takes time to establish new connections between ideas. It takes time to integrate new ideas into one's personal identity and with one's previous understanding of the company's situation. It takes time to test new insight against actual work situations. It takes time to agree on new procedures, and so forth.

As the case studies demonstrate, learning not only takes place during the individual consultation sessions, but also in the working periods in between. This means that *extensive and segmented time* promotes both individual and collective learning.

This, by the way, is not just true for the participants, but also for the consultant, who needs time to think and reflect. What the systemic consultant can do in order to promote her own cognitive processes will be the topic of closer inspection in chapters 6 and 7.

Drawing up the ground rules

Consultations are not only defined in time and space, but are also characterized by the fact that other rules apply here than in the daily work in the organization.

In my experience, it is a good idea—regardless of whether some of the same persons participated both in the initial negotiations and in the first meeting with the participant group—to spend some time on an explicit discussion of the ground rules that apply for the consultation. This can be done in many ways, but is often based on questions, such as: "What ground rules are necessary in order for this consultation to lead to good results?" or "What ground rules do we need—in order to make sure that this is worth while?"

The ground rules that the participants come up with usually have to do with openness, honesty, active listening, a respect for differences and confidentiality in relation to others outside the consultation-room. All of these are important prerequisites for progressions in the collective learning process. Obviously, it is one thing to draw up these rules and quite another to respect them and to trust others to respect them. How difficult this is going to be depends, among other things, on how different these rules seem to be from the daily norms and behaviour in the company. But whether the difference is small or great, it is important to describe the desired reality in words, as this will automatically mobilize efforts towards making it come true. This is only one small example of how consultation can employ the enormous power of positive thinking. (See more about this in, among other places, Cooperrider, 1990.)

Stages in the consultation

Describing the stages of the consultation may be a good device for structuring time and activities, to the benefit of the commissioner, the participants, and the consultant. And indeed, all areas of consultation include several models that are based on stages. These segmented models often employ reasoning from the scientific world, where stages in a research project are described as being logically and rationally separate, containing activities that are separate—and must be held separate—from each other. In scientific research it is important, for example, to keep description and interpretation separate. In systemic consultation, the opposite is closer to the truth, which I will explain below.

Segmented models appear in systemic literature too. Below is a model in seven stages, inspired by Campbell (1995):

Stage 1:   *Referral*
Considerations about the referral: How did it arise? What is the meaning of the referral for the different members of the organization?

Stage 2:   *Learning about the organization and making hypotheses*
What kind of organization is this? What is it like for the employees to work in the organization? What questions need further exploration?

Stage 3:   *Designing the consultation and agreeing on the contract*
The consultant draws up a mutual contract that clarifies the expectations and working methods of the client-system and the consultant.

Stage 4:   *Interviewing to gather data*

Interviews can be carried out in the form of a large meeting or with individuals. The aim is to talk to relevant people to explore different hypotheses of what is going on, and how it should be interpreted.

Stage 5:   *Presenting your ideas*

There are many ways to do this. The consultant may present or invite for ideas in the course of interviewing, in reflecting discussions, or in the form of more formal reports.

Stage 6:   *Planning and incorporation into the organizational life*

Presenting ideas is only the first step in putting them into practice. Assessing the consequences for the organization of any proposed changes should be considered an essential part of the consultation.

Stage 7:   *Exit (of the consultant)*

Some time after the completion of the consultation, a meeting is held with persons in the organization in order to provide assistance with handling the process of change that was triggered by the consultation.

As it will appear from this model, stages in systemic thinking have a more fluid character. The separation between the stages is not as important as in scientific research. The stage model is mostly meant as a guide for the consultant, as a help to ensure that the necessary considerations are made. From one consultation to another, only the initial and final stages (1, 2, 3, and 7) will be the same, whereas there will be great variation in the structuring of the middle part of the time plan for a consultation. The two case studies will illustrate this. To the client-system, the middle part is the most interesting, while it will often be difficult for the referrer and the commissioner to imagine just *how* many considerations are necessary in the initial stages. They will therefore be impatient to "get going", while the consultant feels that the process has already been long underway.

Methodological considerations
and the collective learning process

How do the stages in a consultation relate to the stages in the collective learning process? A scientifically inspired understanding might give the impression that they must be parallel: first a stage where data is generated, then a stage where data is integrated, and so forth. This, however, is not the case. The model for the collective learning process is a tool for the systemic consultant who may use it to consider—in each stage of the consultation—how to create possibilities for going through the stages of the learning process once or repeatedly.

This is true also of the initial contact. Let us consider the first meeting in a potential consultation assignment as an example. Present may be the referrer, the commissioner (a manager), an employee, and the consultant. Within the setting of this meeting—which typically lasts about two hours—a great number of events need to take place in order for the meeting to be successful: the consultant has to establish a good contact with everyone present; everyone has to have a chance to be heard; known information has to be exchanged (concerning the company's situation and the consultant's background); credibility and trust have to be established; and so forth. But the decisive criterion for a successful meeting is whether it creates possibilities for going through the collective learning process. If the meeting is nothing more than an exchange of known information, it is a dull affair. The purpose of the first meeting is to establish a *better* basis for decision-making than the company already had. Here, the systemic consultant's preparations and ability to improvise questions along the way become essential. The challenge is to be able to find the angles and the questions that lead to the generation of information and points of view that are experienced as new and surprising by at least one of the persons present. When this happens, it creates energy, curiosity, and a desire to get involved. Seen in relation to the collective learning process, what happens in these situations is that information from the private meaning structures becomes available for discussion, and the implicit collective meaning structures may be open to investigation as well. The surprise shows in the body language but is often also commented on in statements like, "Really, I had *no* idea!" or "But, you've never mentioned that before!?" One of the ways that new data can be generated is through the consultant's position-related questions: "When did you—as managing director—become aware of the problem?", "When did you—as a member of the staff—first notice the problem?" This makes room for the differences that are often eliminated from everyday discussions.

The consultant's listening skills and interest in different points of view will help prepare the way for Stage 2: integration into the organizational context. Information is transferred between individuals and linked to personal points of view.

The consultant can create possibilities for progressing from Stage 2 to Stage 3 by asking questions concerning the understanding and interpretations that the participants apply to the statements of the others: "If many employees perceive it the way that X does, what impact does that have on . . . ?"

A first meeting should always be concluded with a number of decisions (Stage 4). At a minimum, there should be a joint decision as to whether there is any basis for continued talks about the potential consultation. If this is the case, there has to be an agreement concerning when and how. Or, perhaps, the parties already agree to have a consultation, but they need some time to look into alternative ways of designing and conducting the consultation.

The consultant may think of the first meeting as an interview where the consultant's questions should increase the chances for progression in the collective learning process. The interview is usually the only option at the first meeting, which is usually characterized by the fact that there is no formal or psychological contract yet. The interview is a familiar method, while more "exotic" methods will seem too alien, as long as there is no psychological contract to make them legitimate.

Once the contract has been drawn up and the consultant's latitude for developing and employing various methods has been defined, the repertoire is extensive. The systemic consultant's choice and application of methods will be influenced by considerations as to which progressions in the collective learning process it will be most relevant to work towards. In the beginning, the main emphasis will be on progressions from Stage 1 to Stage 2, the generation *and* dissemination of information and opinions. The systemic consultant will avoid activities that belong only in Stage 1, the generation of data exclusively for the consultant's use (as in expert advice) and without immediate dissemination to the participants. In relation to the collective learning process, the reason for this is obvious: the integration of data into the organizational context can only take place if the data in question become collective property.

Later in the consultation, the main emphasis will be on the progression from Stage 2 to Stage 3. The integration of knowledge within the organizational context and the interpretation of this will often inspire the expression of additional information and opinions, which is why the emphasis on the various progressions has to be relative.

At the end of a consultation, the focus will be on the progression from Stage 3 to Stage 4: interpretation and decisions for action. The systemic consultant will carefully consider where to

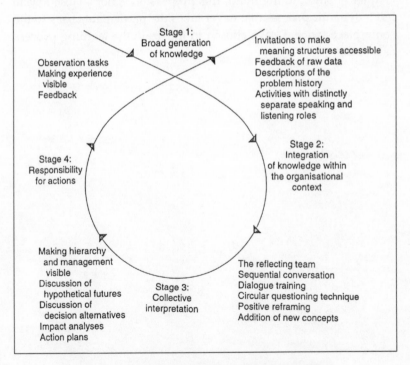

FIGURE 2.5.   The systemic consultant's methods
seen in relation to the collective learning process

draw the line between the considerations about decisions that can only take place within the consultation and those that must be referred to the management system. (See more on this in the section about professional domains in chapter 5.4.)

In a segmented consultation, where there are a number of sessions with working periods in between them (as in both the case studies), there is good opportunity to include the experience from the intermediate working periods. Methods for achieving this will promote the progression from Stage 1 to Stage 4.

It is, thus, an important point that the systemic consultant's methods are created and used with a view to *promoting progression between the four stages in the collective learning process.*

Figure 2.5 provides examples of how this can be achieved. Some of these methods are well-defined, others will need to be created during the consultation. The use of these methods is illustrated in the case studies as well as in a more theoretical context in chapter 5. Since, to my mind, this progression is not a closed cycle but a dynamic process that never takes the participants back to the same place twice, I have chosen to illustrate the learning process as a spiral.

CHAPTER THREE

"Assess our manager
and expose his shortcomings":
a consultation in a private company

Kit Sanne Nielsen

This consultation lasted seven months and took place in a large, private company, for which I have done several assignments over the years. The organization has been disguised, and the names are fictional.

I chose to include this assignment, because it required several intervention levels and was therefore particularly complicated. In addition, it is a practical example of how I use a systemic learning model in my work as a consultant.

The psychological contract allowed a wide array of intervention levels and great freedom in the consultation work. In addition, this assignment developed in unexpected ways, which also contributed to its complexity. The consultation took place on different levels: (1) an individual manager level, (2) a team level, and (3) an organization level, because a new departmental and management structure was established after the assignment had been completed. The initial request dealt with the interaction between management team and employee team, the interaction within the employee team and the interaction between organizational structure and manager. As will

*become apparent, management relations and job satisfaction
played a prominent role, and the case reflects the different
aspects of the management task.*

Case study

The request

The request came from the company's personnel department—an internal human resources consultant for whom I
have worked in the past. The internal consultant called me
and asked if I would be willing to help one of the company's staff
departments with a matter concerning management and cooperation. The consultant explained that for years several staff members
had been unhappy with the way that the department was being
managed, and some of them had, on their own initiative, addressed the issue with the human resources consultant. The complaints said that the manager was weak and evasive and tended to
avoid conflicts at all costs, that he did not establish clear goals for
the employees, and that cooperation between the employees was
fraught with suspicion, internal competition, and cliques. The employees also complained that the manager lacked an overall view
and control of the work plans. The consultant told me that some
members of the staff were talking behind some of their colleagues'
backs and had formed a united front against them.

Since I had worked for this company in the past, I knew the
following:

In this company, the human resources function provides human resources consultants who advise and support the line managers in their human resources development work. For several
years, human resources development has been a vital area in the
corporate development.

One of the company's fundamental values is that it relies on its
human resources. Employee qualifications are an important com-
petitive factor. It is therefore necessary for the line managers to
have responsibility both for the work and for human resources
management. The high priority on human resources management,

however, reduces the line managers' possibility for taking care of operations and work. If the managers, on the other hand, devote a great deal of time to human resources management, there is a risk that the highly qualified and skilled employees feel that the professional aspects of their job do not receive sufficient attention from the manager.

The company's attitude is that employee involvement is essential for the company's success (in terms of market shares and quality), and that it is management's job to create this involvement. Managers are frequently measured on their ability to accomplish this.

The demand for "dialogue-based" human resources management in the company has been rising, and the introduction of several types of management performance evaluations has directed increased attention to the manager's ability for human resources management and problem solving. This is probably an added stress factor for many managers and a "weapon" in the hands of dissatisfied employees.

I should add here that I was not surprised to receive this request. A few months prior to it I had carried out a consultation in an adjacent department, and in this connection I had talked with an employee from the staff department. The employee had applied for a similar position in the neighbouring department. Upon not getting the job, she asked for some personal feedback on her application. During our conversation, she told me that *the very poor working environment in the department* was her main reason for wanting to leave. She gave me a detailed and lengthy description of that situation from the employees' point of view. I remember her telling me that *"I have told our manager that we need a consultant to help us out of our problems, but he is so afraid of conflicts that I doubt if he has the courage"*.

Stage 1: *Initial contract with the manager, John*

John called me and asked for my assistance. He was extremely interested, almost pleading, and used many superlatives in his request for help. We arranged a meeting to talk matters over. The

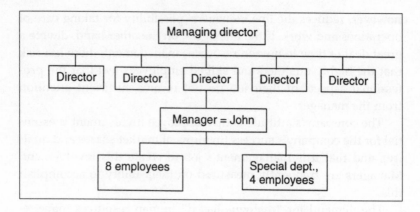

FIGURE 3.1.   Organization chart

initial arrangement was that I would interview him to clarify what
sort of help he wanted, and that we would make an agreement
concerning the assignment and my role in the process.

In the meeting, I asked the manager to tell me what he needed
help with, and why. First, he gave me an introduction to the department's tasks and a brief historical outline of the department's
position in the overall operations of the company (Figure 3.1).
This provided me with a good background for understanding the
job functions of the individual employees and the manager's responsibility concerning the professional aspects of the work. He
then gave me a personal characterization of each employee in the
department (this was his own choice). There were 12 employees,
and he spent 5 minutes on each. One employee, for example, was
characterized as "reliable, stable, responsible, with good listening
skills", another as "really good professional skills, dynamic, entre-
preneurial, ambitious", and so forth. I was impressed with his
great interest in his team members as persons, and I noted a
strong involvement in the employees. He also described their personal relations—who got along well, who helped each other out,
who had a problematic relationship with each other. When I asked
him what he saw as the most pressing problem for us to work on,
he said: "*I wish for everybody to think of this as a good place to work,
but I am afraid that some don't see it that way. I probably have my weak
points that I am not aware of, and—can't you help us see what the
problem is? I think that it will take a neutral outsider to define the*

problem for us. I mean, I see and hear that some people are dissatisfied, but I don't actually see quite what the problem is, and why it has to be this way."

John also told me about a difficult conflict. A year earlier, the department had hired a new, academic employee. During the hiring procedure, there had been a disagreement between John and a group of employees concerning who should be picked among 20 applicants. In the end, John had chosen someone that he considered very qualified—a person whom he knew from before and whom he had encouraged to apply. This had caused considerable discussion among the employees. One "faction" felt that the whole thing had been pre-arranged, and they were furious with what had happened. John had been called dishonest and manipulative. The "new" employee had not yet been fully accepted by certain of his colleagues. They avoided him and made sarcastic comments about him, while others tried to defend him. The new employee, of course, was in a tough spot himself, and he was not a member of any of the "cliques".

As there seemed to be several angles to reaching an understanding of the problems, I suggested to John that we carry out a climate survey. Part of my reasoning for this was that the company had developed this organizational tool itself, and that the department had not yet carried out its own climate survey. Besides, the results of the survey might provide a good point of departure for a debate and an investigation of the problems with the participation of everybody. This would be a good way to begin, as it would lead to a broader generation of knowledge and ideas, which a common discussion could be based on (see chapter 2). John liked the idea. At the end of the meeting, we had drawn up the following action plan together.

We wanted to use the company's own method for carrying out a climate survey. The survey would be processed in the human resources department (it would be an anonymous survey). The computer results were to be read by John and myself, and we would then spend a *theme day* together with the staff to discuss the results and decide on the next steps. John would brief the employees about the meeting we had just had and about the preliminary plan. I was to explain the method in more detail at our meeting with the employees.

If further consultation was needed, this would be decided at the end of the theme day. Qualitative interviews with the employees and a team-building course seemed obvious possibilities.

John was also offered supervision—an offer that he accepted. The supervision was to provide a basis for taking stock of the process together and to aid and support John.

The contract

My contract with John stated the following:

I was to be the chief consultant. I would be given the freedom to choose what methods I deemed appropriate in the process. I was to support John in handling the management task better and provide supervision along the way. The internal consultant, who had handled the initial contact, was to be out of the project in the sense that he would not be receiving information, unless the manager thought it was relevant and wished to include the internal consultant. In that case, the manager would have to contact the human resources consultant himself. In that way, both John and the human resources consultant would be a part of the client-system. I informed the human resources department of this, and John was the one who signed the contract.

Reflections

John had decided to get outside help. I assumed that he had finally caved in after the employees, the human resources consultant, and manager colleagues in the neighbouring department had tried to sell him the idea.

After the telephone conversation, I wondered about his "charm campaign", and I wondered what it might reflect. It was clear that he wanted to make a good first impression. Had he guessed that others had spoken badly of him, and that I already knew these views? Did he know that I knew that other people thought his department was having problems?

What would happen at the meeting? How could I assume a reasonably neutral position and, at the same time, gain John's trust

that I would be loyal to him? What consequences might this potential invitation to form an alliance have to our first meeting? I decided to use the first stage to gather information and to listen. It is
important for a consultant to be able to form alliances with everybody and nobody at the same time. This would be my opening
strategy for my first meeting with him.

My impression after the meeting was that John was unsure about
the actual nature of the problems. His behaviour expressed an
almost humble and pleading style. He expressed a need for ap-
proval and was clearly nervous about the process that he was
about to initiate. He addressed me "Dear Kit" several times, which
I interpreted as a strong desire to get me on his side. Was he
lonesome in his job? Did he need support? I chose to go along as
far as necessary to make it clear to him that I wanted to help him,
but at the same time I made it clear that everyone would have to
be able to speak their mind concerning the state of things in the
department. This later turned out to be a difficult balancing act. In
relation to the theory about professional domains (see chapter 5.4),
I was here clearly in the domain of ethics (also called the domain
of aesthetics, cf. Cronen and Lang, 1990). I had to make my own
personal ethics clear and put myself in a position where I could
remain open and curious while not getting won over by information and views from the various parties. At the same time, I had to
be loyal and understanding towards the difficult position that I
knew John was in. I knew that I had to make it clear from the
beginning that I had to be free to choose the methods, techniques,
and hypotheses that I found useful to my consultation, or I would
not be able to help the system find new ways of acting and cooperating.

Stage 2: *Meeting with manager, assistant manager,
          and staff*

This meeting began with a short, personal presentation of everyone. I briefly explained who I was, described my knowledge of the
company, and gave some examples of typical assignments that I
had carried out for the company in the past. I then suggested that

we begin with a climate survey. I emphasized that everyone was to be included, from the beginning, in describing the job situation, so that, later, everyone would share the responsibility for improving the situation. This was generally received well, although with some reservations. Many people looked relieved, a few people expressed their doubts as to whether this was sufficient, and there was some discussion of this point. I noted the great differences of opinion within the group. After I had explained the method and thematic content of the climate survey, everybody filled in the questionnaire.

I got the impression that the group was interested and prepared to deal with the problems, although some were more motivated than others. Management and cooperation problems had existed for years, and expectations for the outcome varied. Some were eager to get started, others were more reserved and sceptical. A few people felt that this was a waste of time, and that all that was needed was for the manager to put the disgruntled and complaining people in their place. Depending on people's position in the group, they viewed the problem complex very differently.

The questionnaires were returned to the company's human resources department, where the results were calculated by a computer programme.

Stage 3: *The findings of the climate survey*

When I received the findings of the climate survey a few days later, I thought that John must find them pretty shocking. If he had managed to block out the degree of dissatisfaction among his staff, this was a real wake-up call. In his version, the problems had to do with a lack of mutual respect and understanding, but the current findings reflected massive dissatisfaction in every single area that had been investigated. There were major problems concerning clarity of goals, customer orientation, influence on tasks, feedback and acknowledgement, cooperation, conflict-solving, innovation, and so forth.

The employees all had a high level of education, and they would therefore also expect their skills to be put to use and to be able to develop through their job. The negative evaluation might also be interpreted as a sign that people were not getting the challenges and goals to ensure satisfactory development of their skills and qualifications. The participants' replies showed that they needed explicit goals and direction. Disharmony, competition, low motivation, and so forth seemed to be a part of the problem. John and the group now had to decide what conclusions to draw from the survey, and I wondered how open the discussion would be and whether the employees would own up to their criticism when we all met for the theme day.

Reflections

I was aware that this would be a blow to John, and I therefore carefully considered how to discuss things with him. The climate survey spoke very clearly; 92% of the replies fell under the category of "potential problem areas". The severity of the result could be read as a clear signal of dissatisfaction and a demand for change. In that sense the results conveyed an unambiguous message. This matched the information that I had received before the consultation began from my "first informant", the employee who did not get the job that she had applied for. It reflected and confirmed the assumption: the problems had existed for years and on several levels—management, relations, and tasks. As a consultant, I might consider why a group of employees would paint such a bleak picture of their department. Was it a collective attempt at mutiny—sending a loud and clear signal to the company that this manager had to go? Why were the employees so angry/confused/dissatisfied? What had caused this? What conflicts lay behind it? What battles had taken place over the years? Who had lost and won?

Stage 4: *Theme day about the climate survey*

On the theme day, everyone was involved in debating the climate survey. I presented an outline of the findings, and everyone was given a copy of them. Then the team worked in two smaller groups, in which they discussed and ranked the problems. After going over these in the large group, I decided to go one level deeper and try to get an answer to the following questions: How did the individual employee experience the working environment, cooperation, and management on a daily basis? How were things experienced emotionally? I chose to conduct this as an open interview and asked for a volunteer.

The rest of the group participated as a reflective team. The employee who had agreed to be interviewed represented the most outspoken group of dissatisfied employees. She expressed openly, honestly, and directly how matters were influencing her, both personally and professionally. She stated the following:

"I don't see how my work is part of the overall efforts of the department, and I don't feel that our manager is helping me with this in any way. Actually, I am unable to communicate with him at all. Our image to the outside is far too poor, and I don't think that our professional level is up to the standards that the customers have a right to expect. Everything is so messy here, John has just delegated everything, and he never follows up on anything. I have lost my motivation, because there is no development. We have just ground to a halt here. John makes peculiar decisions. He keeps changing his mind, and it is usually the last person who speaks to him that gets it their way!—We lack trust in each other, and there is no real team spirit. We are stuck—no new ideas or goals, and I am getting out as soon as I find another job!"

The team reflected on these statements, and it became a very personal and intense session. In this session there was one person to whom I will refer as the "team's oracle", because she was to be the one to uncover a repressed story. Her disclosure can be summarized as follows:

The department had lost a treasured employee who had been in the department for 25 years, Peter. He had died from cancer a few weeks after his 60th birthday. The entire department had been to his birthday party. The loss was painful, not just for personal and emotional reasons, for the colleagues who had known him for several years; the loss was greater than that. Peter had had the role of "co-ordinator" between management and staff. He was the one who made sure that John passed the appropriate information on to the team. He was the one who told John how things were going in the team. Peter was the one who cleaned up and ordered office supplies when they were used up—indeed, it seemed that Peter had been making up for all the things that now were no longer being taken care of—in terms of practical things and work. He was an organizational communication link between John and the staff—or, as one of the employees put it: I think we all feel bad about this—Peter was the bloody errand-boy for all of us.

Several of the team members were getting misty-eyed during this story. A couple of them cried openly. John was very affected. The story had touched on something that was very deep and painful to many in the group. I was surprised and pensive. I decided to give the group some time to express the feelings that were now coming out. Slowly, there was a change in the group. Some of them put a hand on someone else's shoulder, and some borrowed handkerchiefs from the person next to them. Some of the employees who had sat in silence, listening and watching other people's reactions, spoke up and expressed surprise, emotions, and opinions. Gradually, the atmosphere changed into a sense of sympathetic interest and compassion.

At this point I found it appropriate to intervene with a general hypothesis, which was to serve the purpose of creating insight and emotional relief in the group. The hypothesis, which was developed in stages, can be summarized in the following working hypothesis:

"It appears that Peter was a very valuable person to all of you. He filled a part and took care of a function as the person who picked up the loose ends, cleaned up, provided co-ordination, did the photocopying, sent out the mail, and so forth, and he helped distribute the practical tasks. These jobs have been floating around since then. Some of the jobs have been transferred to the secretaries, who now feel over-burdened because they have to handle all this in addition to their other secretarial duties. Furthermore, Peter helped John communicate with the staff—he acted as John's liaison and coach. He sorted out misunderstandings, gave John advice, and took action when conflicts were underway, acting as an emissary. Of course you miss him. Understandably, some of you still have a hard time with this. But don't you think that Peter was happy with this function, which he both took and was given? Some of you express anger, because he never refused this role as "errand boy". Imagine that Peter was to give you all some good advice today; what would he say?"

The silence in the group was deafening. I then asked the group to separate into smaller teams to reflect on this and provide some ideas on the kinds of thoughts and advice that Peter might have had for them. This assignment led to many thoughts and emotions, and the plenary session later showed that the group was ready for a more action-oriented phase. There were suggestions of drawing up a systematic list of the tasks to be handled, defining who would distribute them in the future. The group session that followed was hardworking and efficient and led to the establishment of a task group to look more closely at the distribution of a number of tasks in order to find a more flexible distribution. This included:

1. secretarial tasks
2. entering data and reporting data
3. repairing and maintaining technical equipment
4. other tasks (for example, traineeships, tidying, telephone complaints, refunding expenses after trips and courses, and so forth).

The task group was to work out a list of the tasks, who was responsible for them, and who would carry them out.

This was the end of the theme day. The feedback at the end of the day was positive. Hopes were expressed that John and the employees would pull together to solve the task as it had been defined. John asked the staff to agree to follow up the theme day with a 3-day seminar, where the group was to define goals and focus areas and continue with a team-building process. The feedback to John led to a wish for a team-building process that would address differences between the employees, give training in direct communication, and establish more respectful relations.

Reflections

The climate survey elicited many signals that the department was lacking job satisfaction. In several areas, the employees felt that relations between management and staff were burdened with suspicion, dissatisfaction, anger, and frustration. The complaints over poor management were clear and overwhelming. Since a dialogue had been established during the theme day, I was hoping that the group had begun to build a better foundation for a viable interaction. We had only touched briefly on John's role and function. He had been criticized, he had dealt with criticism, and perhaps he had a sense that he should take more control of the department. He had delegated many tasks, and he was criticized for not providing sufficient follow-up, but he now had the help of several of his employees. Would he put in an active effort himself? The meaning of Peter's role had been made clear, both to John and to the staff, but what conclusions would they draw themselves, and what changes might it lead to? There were conflicting and repressed feelings and attitudes towards Peter, and apparently the group had kept them hidden for a long time. At least the violent reactions of grief suggested that a dam had broken—and words, tears, anger, and relief flowed freely. Would this episode strengthen the group internally and weaken some of the fronts and alliances that had characterized the group for a year and a half? One of my interventions had been to help the group "bury" Peter and then to motivate them to assume collective responsibility for the "clean-up". I was hoping, of course, that this would prepare the way for a greater degree of shared responsibility, and that this would have a positive effect on the cooperation. The process work on the theme day took place both in the domain of ethics and in the domain of production. The participants had expressed their own moral values and attitudes to the interaction and worked on producing proposals and ideas for new procedures and methods for various organizational tasks. The participants had shown their willingness to work together on defining and agreeing what activities should be given higher priority, and to discuss how they might progress with this systematic, practical work. In the domain of production, clarity is of the essence, and by making the distribution of tasks, responsibility, and authority more explicit, the department could benefit by becoming more productive and efficient. These "virtues" were in demand from the employees, who were ambitious and hardworking. But in order for the department to function as intended, John would have to make the necessary decisions while still being in charge of co-ordination and control in this stage. This was exactly the role that John was being criticized for not filling.

I was wondering how John would react later. Did he feel that the employees were willing to support him in his job as the manager? Or did he fear "the writing on the wall", which might lead to his dismissal? The employees had expressed their criticism and demands. They wanted goals, clear areas of responsibility, procedures, and management, and to me they seemed willing to share the responsibility. I was not sure whether John saw things the same way, and whether he intended to assume leadership now during this process of change. Did he have the necessary qualifications? Did he have the will? Did he want to? My next supervision meetings with him would provide the answer. He appeared to be open and responsive, but did he also have the will to participate in changing the way things worked? He had expressed his interest and good intentions, but was he able to live up to that? I had my doubts and decided to find the answers to some of these questions.

It was my impression that the group had been dysfunctional for a while. The impression I had of the group suggested the following: There was a basic lack of a joint and collective team spirit. There were sporadic signs of a team spirit, but only in subgroups, and there was considerable confusion as to the goals of the group and how they should be reached by the group as a team. Rules, leadership, influence, and responsibility were drifting, and some of the group members were not sure that they would be accepted into the group. Others had found a social group where they felt secure, and where they felt a sense of belonging. Some individuals got along in a rule-governed group climate, where emotions were not discussed, and work-related subjects were the only ones allowed. Many were unhappy with John as a manager. Some tried to cover for him. The big differences had polarized the group, which needed a common vision and group identity. The unclear leadership made the group unable to handle differences in personalities and opinions, aspects that were necessary in order to develop a productive and functioning group.

The intermediate stage

During the next stage, the established work group worked on structuring and distributing tasks. The progression and implementation of this work appeared to be relatively unproblematic, and the effect was an internal solidarity within the staff group, where areas of responsibility and authority were made explicit. I noticed that it was easier for the staff and for John to cooperate in the domain of production than to cope with the differences in the domain of ethics. Both in the following meetings with the manager and from minutes of the departmental meetings, which were sent to me, I could see that this work was proceeding according to plan and apparently without any great problems. The manager expressed his satisfaction with the process.

There were, however, still some areas that needed to be sorted in the distribution of responsibility between the manager and the assistant manager, so I met with them a couple of times in order to help them define and describe a clearer distribution of work between them.

Stage 5: Interview stage

The staff wanted me to interview all employees before the following seminar. An interview stage had been included in the contract as a possibility, if the staff and John found it to be relevant, and it would give everybody an opportunity to elaborate on the findings of the climate survey with qualitative statements on how management and cooperation was perceived. Everybody was interviewed one to one (except for a special group of four people who chose a group interview). These interviews provided a great deal of information about the department's culture for cooperation, attitudes, likes and dislikes, alliances, personal frustrations, and the "skeletons in the closet". The employees got some things off their chest and, to some extent, underwent a "detoxification". It was a great benefit that everybody felt that they had been heard, listened to, and understood, and it gave me the opportunity to formulate new hypotheses to provide a point of departure for the planning of the coming seminar. The interview round also allowed me to formulate systemic questions in connection to the interviews for the staff members and John to reflect on at the upcoming seminar.

A recurrent element in the views of the employees had come up in the interviews:

The company's top management had not been showing much interest in the output of the department. But lately there had been more focus on what the department should deliver, and how. The "internal customers" in the company felt that the department was acting on a wish to control other departments in the company, and that they did not provide the guidance and feedback to other departments that were expected of it. The customers did not feel that they were getting the service they required and instead tried to avoid contact with the department. Therefore they were not making demands on the quality of the department's services. This had a de-motivating effect on the department staff. In an innovative and performance-oriented company culture, this had caused others not to appreciate the department and its services. From a company perspective, this obviously had a negative influence on the self-esteem of the employees in the department. The employees could not tell whether it was because of this situation, or whether it was due to the internal problems, but in any case the effect was that John and his employees felt stuck and therefore had difficulties developing. They lacked innovation, spirit, and involvement. One of my hypotheses was that this had caused a build-up of energy that expressed itself through negativity, stress, and frustration with the lack of challenges and development.

Reflections

In my interpretation of the interview findings, the group in the special section seemed to function well internally. But they were tired of participating in the common departmental meetings and witnessing what they referred to as the bickering in the department. The special section tended to watch things from the sidelines, as they were geographically located in other buildings and only went to the main building occasionally. This group enjoyed the cooperation with John and felt that he provided "professional input". Their relationship with him differed from that of the other employees in the main section, because they answered to a different manager on a daily basis. They had a number of interesting observations. They felt that John's greatest difficulty was that he practised "individual management instead of group management". John liked to talk things over in the corridor with whomever he ran into, instead of in a common forum. He made many special deals with people "at random" (and was it really at random?), and he did not treat his subordinates equally. This caused irritation and created internal competition. But, at the same time, many in the group also felt that the rest complained too much and were unfair to John. They thought that he should stand up to the people who were complaining. They were somewhat annoyed that he did not face up to more confrontations with the people who complained.

The interviews enabled me to define several intervention levels. It was necessary to address:

1. the manager's responsibility and role
2. the team work and making the group's own resources visible
3. setting up goals for specific tasks and defining the department's *raison d'être* (mission–goals–strategy)

The department had initiated this last process before I came into the picture, and it was clearly something that they wanted to continue to work on.

I therefore decided to open the seminar with the following questions:

• What sort of management does the group want?
• What are the demands and expectations?
• How does one communicate in order to understand other people?
• What differences are there? And how are they utilized?

- What resources does the group possess? And how might the group work towards utilizing these resources?
- How does the group intend to proceed in order to make its mission and strategy visible to the company and the customers?

In my opinion, the participants needed to look at themselves instead of always looking at others.

The climate survey had been an anonymous process, and I now wanted every single employee to be included and made responsible in the continued process.

I also knew that negative stereotypes can be eliminated, once people begin to understand why other people act the way they do. Projections are toned down, when the motivations of other personality types are made explicit. Everything becomes less mysterious, and one recognizes oneself as well as others. This makes it possible to accept other people's motives and preferences. In my experience, such a team process could provide the basis for greater respect and understanding. When one accepts and understands one's own preferences and aversions, one is more likely to understand that others have similar feelings.

Stage 6: *Three-day seminar*

The tool I chose to use as my foundation was the Myers–Briggs Type Indicator (MBTI), which I have used successfully in team-building activities (Myers & Myers, 1993). I began by giving an introduction to different types of personalities and their preferences. Then I gave the group a number of exercises with the purpose of illustrating how people prefer to use different psychological dimensions in different ways. The group turned out to comprise many different personality types.

After this, the group was given a number of tasks to demonstrate what this meant to their cooperation within the team. This gave the participants an opportunity to discuss their own preferred styles of communication and what each of them looked for in a job.

This was the cause of much levity in the group. Great energy can be mobilized by becoming aware of the differences between one's own preferences and those of others; and as it was demonstrated at the same time that all types have their inherent resources and possibilities, many of the participants discovered that everyone could contribute in some way.

The process demonstrated that the previous form of cooperation in the group had been an "either/or" situation. This was discussed openly, and gradually the participants themselves developed a wish towards a greater degree of tolerance and acceptance of many different ways of being, acting, and thinking. This discussion and awareness meant that the manager's personality type and management style could be discussed openly. John's type was different from the majority of the people in the department. John preferred to use an enthusiastic, harmony-seeking and process-oriented style. He thrived on juggling several activities at the same time and tried to keep as many possibilities open as possible. Many of the members of staff expressed a need for a far more structured management style, where John would stick to his choices and decisions. He had delegated *everything*, but had neglected the follow-up. This caused irritation, anger, and confusion.

John and the assistant manager got an opportunity to alter the distribution of responsibility between them. When they presented the outcome, the employees provided feedback and ideas for the plan, and it was agreed and written down how the future planning was going to take place, after the seminar had ended. The roster that the work group had drawn up was also negotiated and co-ordinated with John and the assistant manager.

At the end, everybody had a chance to provide and receive feedback. The result was a dialogue that included everybody and which had produced positive contributions and constructive proposals for changes in the individual participant's own working style and cooperation style.

The last day of the seminar was spent on a debate about goals. John presented the company's overall vision and strategy, and in a later session the participants worked in groups on articulating the department's own goals and focus areas. The following questions were addressed: How should our services change and improve in the future? What are the most important aspects to stress in relation to our customers? Which projects should we finish? Which should we launch, and which should we abandon?

In conclusion, the staff agreed that cooperation was to be handled differently now. It was decided to give high priority to cross-functional projects and to establish project groups on the basis of interests and differences in personality types. As a final step, the goals were to be presented to the managing director. The staff themselves stated that they wanted to include the managing director in order to demonstrate that the department was now actively engaged in moving forward.

In the debate about goals everybody had been active and motivated. Once the individual participants understood their own preferences (needs), they also had more respect for other people's preferences. The work group that had been established was to continue to work on proposals for action plans. The work group was assembled on the basis of the group members' different types. John was a member of the work group.

Reflections

I chose to use *reframing* in the process, because it may introduce new ideas about problem definitions and make new actions possible. Positive reframing is a form of paraphrasing, where negative statements (which are usually inhibiting) are changed into constructive and challenging statements (which are usually motivating and enhancing). The reframing consisted in my constant focus on the group's resources and possibilities by using the Myers–Briggs Type Indicator and asking positive questions concerning the difficulties that the participants experienced during the seminar. For example, I would ask: "How can each of you contribute to . . ." or "How would you like things to be?" I also simplified the problem complex in order to make it more manageable for the group (to eat an elephant, one must cut it into bite-size pieces). This way, large complexes were turned into smaller units, which could be handled step by step (this also made it easier for the group to act, because 80% of the group members preferred practical and concrete directions). Another intervention on my part was to stimulate the participants to relate to the future and avoid spending any more time in the troublesome past. I felt that it was important to the rest of the process that the group "land" in an atmosphere of trust and optimism. The new project groups that sprang from the debate about goals were made up of people who differed in terms of their preferences, and who had previously had a strained relationship. The values that the group wanted to preserve had to appear stable and express "the good things from the past" as opposed to "the bad things from the past".

There was great pressure on John to add new areas of responsibility to his tasks.

The employees had had an opportunity to express their expectations to the leadership—and the ensuing dialogue had specified the new management mandate.

Stage 7: *The period after the seminar*

After the seminar, my supervision of John continued for about two months. We had an agreement that I was to participate in a departmental meeting where the managing director was present. At this meeting, the department was to present its goals and focus areas to the managing director, who would then discuss them with the group. We agreed that John would brief the managing director on what the seminar had accomplished. The managing director was interested in discussing the department's goals for the coming period, and he was invited for this part of the meeting exclusively.

John had kept me up to date and told me that the staff was more active, and communication had improved noticeably. He had his doubts, however, as to whether he had the managing director's support. He was not sure what the source of the managing director's scepticism was. His guess was that, perhaps, the managing director was not sure if John was strong enough to be the manager of the department and maintain the positive trend. John also said that he lacked support and dialogue from the managing director. John felt it difficult to ask for the managing director's support, since the relationship between the managing director and himself had always been formal and impersonal. John felt that he would be able to handle things on his own at this point, and we agreed to end the consultation.

Epilogue

Through a colleague who was an external consultant, I later happened to learn the following:

About two months after the last departmental meeting at which I was present, the company did a management-level reshuffle. John was relieved of his managerial duties and made senior project manager on a specific project. John's department merged with an adjacent department, and the manager of this department was now also the manager of John's department. The new manager had proved to be a structured organizer so far, with good abilities regarding control, coordination, and development. The managing director and the top management were confident that he would be able to continue the development process in the department and create stability and commitment—two things that were *very* important to the organization.

John responded to his demotion with grief, but he held his head high. It was a personal defeat for him, after 20 years as manager of the department. He had valued the prestige and authority that came with formal leadership. As time went by, he learned to accept his situation. When I ran into him in the company, about a year later, he looked far more relaxed and at ease, and he said that he was doing well now. It had been a difficult period, but he was relieved not to have to handle a stressful management position any longer. He was rid of all the hassle now, as he put it, and was able to focus on the non-administrative projects that had actually always held his greatest interest.

The staff members, by and large, were happy about the change. The core tasks were getting more attention, and there was follow-up on current projects. On the other hand, the department might still split into two camps when major changes occurred. This reflects the great extent to which culture determines the behaviour of the members of an organization.

A systemic model of learning

During this consultation I used several methods to help my client-system change the situation. My choice of methods, however, depends on the client-system's view of its own problems. Therefore, the choice of methods is subject to the problem definition. One thing is what the involved persons in the client-system want help with altering; it is quite another what I, as the consultant, perceive to be the need—that is, how I interpret the different parties' perception of the problem. And a third issue is whether we, in cooperation, are able to create new, different, more creative ideas for solving the problem, in order to make it *exciting* to change the problematic situation. A fourth issue is whether the consultant, together with the client-system, is able to create new perceptions of the problems. This can be accomplished, for example, by perceiving the problems as resources, as beneficial and natural means of interacting in the organization, while still actively supporting the idea that, naturally, there may be other ways of interacting.

1. *The generation of knowledge:* The first stage in investigating the understanding of the problem in this case was to gather information about what the department wanted help with (see Figure 3.2). I obtained this information partly through my telephone conversation with the internal consultant and partly through my first conversation with John. Later, information was gathered through the climate survey and the individual interviews.

2. *The integration of knowledge:* John's and the staff members' mental images and their emotional experience of the work situation were made more explicit during the theme day. During the theme day, the findings were given back to the client-system, and the participants were given an opportunity to reflect on their various ways of understanding the problem. Here they were invited into a space where they could communicate about common and individual opinions about the problems. In addition, a space was created where the participants could let out forgotten and repressed stories from the past. Through the use of a circular interview form, supplemented

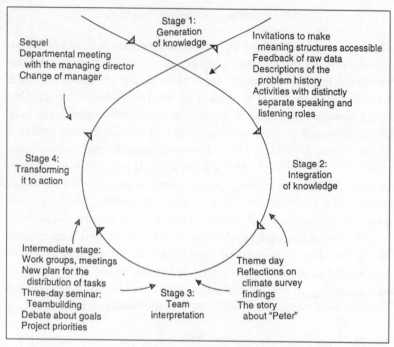

FIGURE **3.2. Model of learning**

with the use of reflecting teams, we were able to uncover the story about Peter. At the same time, if we view it in terms of the learning spiral (see chapter 2), the process progressed from Stage 1 to Stage 2, because learning took place that was influenced by the different mental images of the individual staff members. By listening and by understanding how others perceive the situation and the past, the individuals expanded their perception. This, in turn, created new points of insight that gave the group new possibilities for understanding their common situation. The transition from Stage 1 to Stage 2 on the theme day had happened in a dynamic flow that moved both backwards and forwards in the learning spiral.

3. *Thematic interpretation:* This stage began during the theme day and continued through the entire process. The intermediate stage, where the team work assumed practical form with the systematic distribution of responsibility and management control (controlled by the staff), provided good opportunity for

testing new ways of cooperating and new relations. During this theme work, the staff members experienced new sides of each other, and the sub-groups that had existed in the department were loosened up to some extent. In terms of the learning spiral, this stage lay between the third and the fourth stage, as it was clearly centred around action and debate concerning which organizational tasks should belong to which functions and persons. The three-day seminar, too, was a process that stimulated this stage. The group gained new knowledge about types (Myers–Briggs Type Indicator) and got the opportunity to work with this tool, enabling them to reflect on the implications of their new knowledge. Opportunities were created for giving and receiving feedback from one's colleagues, and the manager's role and responsibility were debated. The debate about goals resulted in the definition of project priorities, and John and the group agreed to include the managing director.

4. *Transforming knowledge to action:* The transition to the fourth stage took place in the period after the seminar and during the sequel. It was during this phase that we would see whether it all held water. Often, the external consultant is no longer involved at this stage, partly because the groups are responsible for implementing the plans and establishing new relations, and partly because most organizations wish to get by on their own without the consultant. Obviously, money is also an issue. According to my information about this stage, however, John did not, in the long run, manage to elicit sufficient trust from top management for him to develop and strengthen his leadership. The department got a new manager, and apparently the staff was rather happy with this change. John was given a new position in the department—a position that he later seemed happy with.

The question, of course, remains: What did John learn? What did the staff learn? What sort of learning took place in the organization? The first two questions would probably be the easiest to answer, provided the consultant had had an opportunity to ask them (I did not!). It is therefore easier to answer a fourth question: What did I learn as a consultant?

The consultant's final reflections

I had given John and the staff the help and a running start for the department to move on, as had been agreed. My job was mostly to prepare the way for more open communication among the members of the staff and between John and the staff. This had been accomplished, in the sense that a better climate had been achieved, a more flexible and tolerant atmosphere, as well as space for individual staff members' skills and interests. Employee motivation increased in the period during and after the consultation.

In my assessment of the effect on the work itself, I concluded that the reconstruction of the distribution of tasks clarified the responsibility for various tasks. These changes created a greater sense of solidarity in the group.

John's managerial responsibilities were clarified in the process, and the employees articulated their expectations for the kind of leadership that they could get behind. This also made it clear where John's management difficulties lay. In this connection, John's boss became aware how big the problems in the department were, and that these cooperation difficulties had existed for years. I interpreted the managing director's management reshuffle as a demonstration that he supported the staff and sided with them. In doing so, he also demonstrated that he had no confidence in John's abilities to exercise leadership.

Personally, my biggest challenge was to avoid assessing whether or not John was a good manager, and to keep my personal opinions to myself. Time and again I was asked to speak my mind, by the internal consultant, by certain employees, and by the managing director. It requires great flexibility, skill, and tact to evade invitations of this sort. The art is *to be able to reflect and ask hypothetical questions instead of answering the questions*.

This may be interpreted as uncertainty and shiftiness, especially by top executives who are looking for quick answers, so that they can make quick decisions. Here, the consultant must stick to her contract with the commissioner or establish a new one, perhaps with top management, where the context and relations are defined. The consultant must refer to her *professional right to remain silent* about the information that the client-system has provided. The consultant must maintain that she is not present as an expert advisor but as a systemic consultant and a process consultant, and she may have to explain to top management or to the internal consultant what this entails. In my personal experience, this is accepted, as long as I maintain my *authoritative right* to define this role. Top managers understand the language of professional authority. It is essential for the organizational consultant to be able to argue this position.

Putting systemic concepts into practice

In the case, I used systemic concepts and methods, and I summarize some of these briefly here.

The circularity in the consultant's understanding of the events

When the consultant is to form a picture of what is going on in the organization, she may view the participants' stories, experiences, and thoughts on the basis of their different observations and positions. Often the stories of the members of the organization are linear—that is, the individual has formed his own logical and unambiguous explanation of what goes on in the organization, and why. When the consultant allows herself to move around more freely within these different stories, the perspectives are expanded, and, thus, the circular understanding is introduced into the consultant's understanding of the events (see also chapter 5.2). The events in the case can be viewed from several different vantage points, and here I want to point to three: (1) John, the manager, (2) the team, and (3) the managing director.

1. John, the manager

It soon became clear to me that John, the manager, felt his own managerial role to be problematic. He strongly doubted whether he was able to satisfy his staff and provide the support and direction that they needed. He was also concerned that others attributed motives to him that he did not feel were really his. In addition, he expressed that his relations with the employees were made difficult because he was too close to some and too distant from others. The different qualities of the relationships made him unable to treat the staff members fairly. His leadership position assumed the nature of alliances with particular employees, which favoured some employees and made others feel rejected. In systemic thinking, we consider it essential for the consultant to be able to move freely within the client-system, an ally to everyone and no one at the same time. In parallel to this, one might say that the manager should make sure to treat everybody as equal partners in the work context. This does not mean treating all employees the same. Employees are different, both as persons and as professionals. It is the manager's job to take these differences into consideration and to utilize them, so that everyone gets to bring their unique human and professional qualities to the department and to the tasks. Equality relates to the domain of ethics (see p. 116), because it expresses the moral view that all employees are of unique importance and value in the organization.

2. *The team*

John's lack of clarity about his own role as a manager is easier to understand when one considers his personal experience in relation to the problem areas that were uncovered within the employee team. In the team there was a similar lack of clarity about various members' competencies, responsibilities, and influence. This was the cause for competition between members. Although it was never stated explicitly, there was an ongoing competition about who was best at carrying out especially the sought-after tasks. A number of work areas had not been made clear by the manager. Who, for example, had the most experience with and knowledge about customer expectations? What was the level of ambition that the department sought to live up to? How was the individual supposed to interact with the others in the group? How were tasks to be divided among the various professional groups? And so on. The fact that the manager was not able to negotiate and determine this together with the staff in their daily work sparked power struggles, conflicts, and jealousy among the team members. There were too many unresolved issues in the daily work (the domain of production: see p. 117). No time had been devoted to negotiating the collective contract between the manager and the staff, a negotiation that should take place continuously, because the work situation changes all the time. These and other unspoken conflicts of interest were circulating in the team, causing the team to divide into subgroups as well as causing internal power struggles within the team. In these conflicts, the team members pulled John's strings, making him bend over backwards to satisfy the different participants—frequently to the detriment of the working environment as well as of the manager himself.

3. The managing director

Viewing this scenario through the managing director's eyes, we are able to discover a number of things. First of all, the director was annoyed that John was unable to secure order and a peaceful working environment in his department. He chose, however, to close his eyes to this fact. At least, he had not been very involved in the internal affairs of the department. His interest lay more with the overall goals seen from a larger company perspective. As a result of this, he did not establish a good-enough contact with John about the day-to-day operations in the department, and he was not very supportive or dialogue-oriented. There may be several explanations of this. Top managers often assume the role as coach to the lower-level managers. In many cases, this may actually prevent problems and increase the efficiency of the management's efforts.

Analysing the case from these different vantage points, thus, makes it easier to see how the levels are intertwined and together work to maintain the system, for good as well as for bad. Solving the problems therefore requires changes on other levels too. When John, for example, no longer held the management position, a new departmental structure was introduced, and the following year the managing director was replaced by another person.

About using different tools within a systemic framework

In the case, I used a number of different methods and two particular tools (climate survey and a Jungian tool, the Myers Briggs Type Indicator). This leads to the question: how can a consultant use other psychological tools and still work as a systemic consultant?

Through their own learning, many consultants have acquired many different methods and tools, at great benefit to their clients. So one might ask: why replace these and start over with something new (the systemic tool)? In our experience, one can easily employ many good learning methods within a systemic framework. To us, systemic thinking constitutes the overall framework and the understanding of individuals and organizations that we have practised and felt inspired by for years. But we have also learned much from other psychological and organizational theories. The basic ideas in systemic thinking, however, provide an excellent framework for working with people in an organizational context. We help the client-system change human relations by making the formal system and the different positions explicit, as we work with the importance of utilizing differences. We use hypotheses as a basis for initiating new actions. In our experience, it is a good idea to include and combine other tools. This is often where we find the nourishment for our creativity and for inventing new ways of doing things. In this ongoing work process, we generate new learning for ourselves and for our clients. We are in many ways "irreverent" towards the tools, and we adapt them to the systemic framework that we have chosen. We use these tools to highlight the systemic points.

Climate surveys can be used in a normative and linear fashion: to nail down reality and point to specific causes (for example, it is management's fault, they alone have caused the problems). In *linear thinking, every problem has one correct cause and solution.* It is, however, possible, to interpret climate surveys in a circular fashion: as an expression of how various participants perceive the work conditions. The answers in a climate survey may be interpreted as the different messages of the participants, thus constituting communication directed at others (management or the consultant). The consultant can use these messages in forming hypotheses about the work conditions. The consultant may then, through her hypotheses, rephrase the answers to make them more positive and constructive. Used in this way, problem areas can be put into a solution-oriented perspective and, subsequently, used as a basis for further investigations. That is actually what happened in this case, where I offered a consultation to the group on the theme day (see p. 47) to explore the meaning of the answers in the climate survey.

The tool *MBTI* focuses on differences in personality types and on people's preferences for various actions. This detailed treatment of differences in personality types often makes it clear to the participants that differences are important and valuable. Such carefully designed processes set the individual free and enable him to make his own competencies—as well as his need for the competencies of others—explicit. This makes it possible to form new relationships that have a positive effect on teamwork.

The consultant's own window to the world: the value of using hypotheses

For the consultant to influence the client-system and work progressively towards the future, she needs to reflect on her observations, thoughts, feelings, and intuitive notions. The consultant, thus, enters directly into a meta-position. By reflecting about her observations, the consultant finds images and contributions that can be used to stage new contexts. The consultant's conclusions are working hypotheses, which express her interpretation of the events. By combining the factual aspects with the experience of being an *observer* to the client-system, the consultant is able to form new understandings of and approaches to the case. The hypotheses serve as feedback for the system, and the participants, then, hopefully, come up with new questions and obtain a *bird's eye view* of the stories.

The working hypotheses, which the consultant uses to grasp the case, are the exclusive property of the consultant. The consultant may choose to make them explicit and give them back to the client-system, or she may choose not to. She has to consider carefully before she decides to do one or the other. She has to consider the ethical aspects of giving it back and attempt to assess the consequences that the message may have for the individual participants and their positions. The consultant must make sure not to damage the hierarchy and, for example, further discredit the manager to the staff. The consultant has to protect the system's weaker members and must avoid siding with any one person or group. If the consultant decides to make her hypotheses explicit, they should be flexible as well as conducive to positive changes. The consultant also has to avoid criticizing the client-system, since everybody has done their best in the given situation—regardless of the fact that their behaviour may have made things difficult for others.

Working hypotheses represent the consultant's internal dialogue about the system's difficulties and resources. They help produce new approaches and create methods and activities in the meeting with the client-system. Through her hypotheses, the consultant can define the context within which she wants to create interventions, and she can choose whether or not to share her reasons for choosing particular methods with the client-system. My experience is that if there is a high degree of uncertainty, anxiety, or resistance to dealing with the problems within the client-system, then one should only provide limited information about one's experiences and intentions. By limiting her feedback and leaving room for the participants' own contributions instead, for example, by asking questions (based on her hypotheses), the consultant makes the participants the active party.

In the case described above, I mostly kept my hypotheses to myself, but in the beginning of the process I chose to present a hypothesis about the role that a late colleague had had in the group (see p. 49). I explained my methods, but not what had made me select these particular ones over others. I knew that there was an expectation in the department to view the *consultant as an expert*. This allowed me to do as I saw fit, which was successful exactly because the participants had positive expectations of my professional competence! The client-system in fact expected me to have a better grasp of the situation than I felt I actually had at times. But my reflections and hypotheses were a good help for me in this process. Systemic thinking and the systemic approach enable the consultant to wonder and ask questions—without knowing the answers. We leave it to the client-system to answer the questions and reflect on them. This sets the consultant free to move within the system and to create new conditions for action.

"Free us from the past!": a consultation in a municipality

Gitte Haslebo

This chapter describes a consultation that lasted five months from the initial request to the final seminar. Some aspects of the factual information have been altered to make it impossible to identify the municipality in question. The names, too, are fictional. I have met the problem areas mentioned here in several guises, in both public and private companies. Many readers are therefore likely to feel that they recognize the story. The reason I chose to include this assignment is an increasing number of requests from managers needing external assistance for handling difficult situations, where they have found themselves at an impasse. Part of the background often turns out to be that strong interpersonal conflicts get tangled up with organizational changes and assume a prominent position in the problem complex. These types of assignments can be difficult for the consultant to handle, too. This is exactly why it is so important to make the key concepts explicit and to develop and improve the methods. This consultation was carried out by a team comprised of a fellow consultant and myself.

Case study

The request

The request came from Janice, who was acting manager of a team of social workers in the department of social affairs and health in a medium-sized municipality. A psychologist, whom she knew from before, had given her the name of my colleague. In the first telephone conversation, Janice explained that her predecessor, Esther, had quit after a very stormy series of events that had lasted just over a year. Janice told my colleague that there had been severe conflicts, and that some of the staff members were still affected by it. Now the group wanted help to deal with these events, which had been hard on many of them and which had caused the team to get "stuck in the past".

The request was followed up with a meeting at the board, where the head of the board (Thomas), Janice, and the chief assistant (Beth) were present. My colleague interviewed them about the traumatic events. Beth explained that the conflict had existed especially between Esther and some members of the staff who felt that her management style was very unpleasant. She had her favourites among the staff, while the rest often felt unjustly criticized. Sometimes employees would walk out in tears, and absenteeism was soaring. To make matters worse, Esther was considered professionally incompetent in relation to the cases that the team was handling. The team had tried to take up the issue with the head of department, but did not feel that he had provided sufficient support and assistance.

The head of department said that he was aware that the team had been having problems, but that he had thought that the problems had become manageable after Esther had resigned and Janice had been made acting manager. The position was now advertised as vacant, and the selection procedure had just begun.

Janice related her first impressions of the team and said that she had conveyed their wish for assistance to the higher levels of management. Management had accepted the request and had offered to provide an external consultant. The consultant, however, had offered them a method course, which the team had rejected. The team wanted help to talk about what had really happened (which they were unable to do on their own), and they wanted help to move on. There had been some improvement, but still, when the team experienced extraordinary pressure, the crisis-related reactions reoccurred (tears, arguments, absenteeism).

My colleague concluded that the assignment would require two consultants, and he would therefore find a colleague who could take it on at short notice. Once a suitable consultant had been found, a non-committal meeting would be held with the team of social workers, who would then be free to accept or reject a new offer. After the meeting, the organization chart and job descriptions were mailed to my colleague.

This was when my involvement began. At my first meeting with my colleague, we went over the papers we had received. These papers made it clear that there was an additional level of management, which had not been represented at the meeting. This was Paul, the head of office, to whom the four team leaders, including Janice, answered.

The organization chart is shown in Figure 4.1.

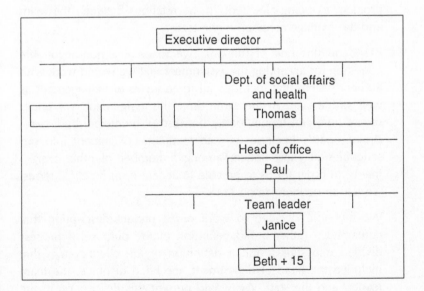

FIGURE 4.1. Organization chart

Reflections

We first considered the aspect that we found the most puzzling: why precisely now? It had been almost a year since the previous team leader, Esther, had resigned. What lay behind the team's decision to define itself as dysfunctional and in need of external assistance? How could we best interpret the fact that the head of office, Paul, was not only absent from the meeting, but was never even mentioned by the others?

How should we handle management's idea that it was primarily the team that had a problem? Maybe this meant that management expected us to work only with the team? This became the basis for our first working hypothesis: Maybe the problem is best handled if we see it in a larger organizational context? Maybe we were not just dealing with a dysfunctional team, but with a dysfunctional management system, where (at least) three levels of management—head of department, head of office, and team leader—had already been involved, to no avail. The head of department—and perhaps also the team leader—seemed to think that the problem was located in the team. Our notion, however, was that it may be more productive to imagine the problem as being "located" in the relations between the team and the management above the team.

Based on this line of thinking, we made it a non-negotiable condition for accepting the assignment that we would work with a client-system that included all three levels of management as well as the staff. At the same time, the assignment was under severe time constraints, partly because of municipal budget restraints, partly because we had to fit the assignment into our schedules at short notice, among a number of other assignments. In order for us to be able to accept it, in practical terms, we had to economize on time.

We therefore decided to work out a project description that contained a rather broad definition of the purpose, a process divided into stages, and a definition of the client-system that included the head of department, the head of office, the team leader, and the staff. We would present this description at the meeting with the team, and if there was any basis for proceeding, we would forward it to the management.

The most important reason that we chose to draw up a project description at such an early stage was our impression that we were dealing with an organization that had trouble reaching decisions. An early project draft would probably make the decision-making easier. Secondly, we wanted to be particularly careful in our efforts to establish a psychological contract. In this connection we were considering the team's past experiences of feeling let down by management and then receiving an offer of help, which the team had rejected.

We therefore planned a meeting with the team of social workers, where we would let the individual participants tell their story and relate their understanding of the problem and their desire for help. Then we would present the project draft and elaborate on our thoughts concerning the draft. The idea was to initiate a process already at the first meeting with the team, in which the exchange of different versions of the story would be possible (see end of this chapter).

Stage 1: *Establishing a psychological and formal contract*

Non-committal meeting with the caseworker team

Janice and twelve of the staff members participated in the meeting, while four were absent that day. We suggested a round to let each person explain how long he or she had worked in the department, how he or she perceived the problem, and what he or she felt was needed in order for the team to move on. There turned out to be substantial differences within the team, concerning both the current impact of past events and the perceived severity of these events. Many expressed a lack of trust in the management, feelings of having been let down, and a lack of conviction that the management had learned anything.

Many concerns and questions were expressed, such as: Why had it been so difficult? Why had management not been willing to

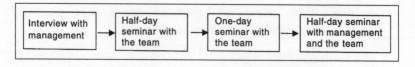

FIGURE **4.2.**   **The process in stages**

listen to the team? Could the same thing happen again? What had been said behind closed doors? Had Esther said anything negative about the individual members of staff to Thomas and Paul, so that they now had minus-points in "the little black book", which they themselves were unaware of and unable to defend against? Could the past be used against them? Why had Esther been given the position in the first place? Did management agree that she was incompetent? Did management recognize the qualifications of the team members? And so forth.

After summarizing the main themes we had heard in the many statements, we presented the two-page project draft.

We defined the purpose as "creating a dialogue about the process that the team has been through for the past year and a half, with a view to dealing with the difficulties in that process and releasing energy for the team's future development and work".

The project draft proposed the process shown in Figure 4.2.

The team expressed a mixture of surprise, anxiety, and satisfaction with our decision to include both Thomas and Paul. The meeting ended with an agreement that the team would go on to discuss whether it would accept our offer, and that we would be informed of the team's decision the following day.

The next day Janice contacted us to say, on behalf of the team, that they would like to use us as consultants.

Reflections

It made a big impression on us that the team was directing so much attention and energy—mostly in the form of negative feelings—at the management levels above Janice. We were seeing the contours of a parallel problem: Whereas Thomas wanted us to "fix" the team, to make it function better and the members thrive more, at least part of the team wanted us to "fix" the management, either by educating it to become more caring or by agreeing with the team that the management was, to some extent, incompetent.

This led to our second working hypothesis: *Maybe we are faced with a client-system where communication between the organizational levels is so limited that it is difficult for the individual to change perspective and imagine how reality looks from a different vantage point?* If this was the case, it could increase the tendency to see everything in black and white, which would reduce the team's capacity for problem solving.

This hypothesis made it even clearer to us that it would be difficult for us to achieve equally good connections with all parts of the system. We were worried that we might already have committed a blunder by presenting the draft to the team before presenting it to the management. Our concern was that by forming an alliance with the team that was stronger than our alliance with management we might have jeopardized our neutrality. The coming events would show to what extent this was the case.

Signing the contract

After our meeting with the team of social workers, we expanded the time we planned to spend with the management and the team a little and added a description of the ground rules. We then sent the project description with no further changes to Janice, our contact person. It came back with Thomas's signature.

The project description contained, as already mentioned, the purpose, plan, and ground rules, but not the contents and methods, which would be determined on the basis of the feedback throughout the process. The following activities were involved:

1. a joint interview with the head of department, head of office, and team leader (2 hours)
2. a half-day seminar with the team aiming at defining the problem and specifying the team's need for assistance (3 hours)

3. a one-day seminar with the team to work on the themes that had come up during the half-day seminar (7 hours)

4. a seminar with the head of the board, the head of department, the team leader, and the staff (4 hours)

The entire consultation had to be completed in a month.

We found it necessary to begin with a careful definition of the ground rules that we felt should apply to us as consultants, including confidentiality concerning the statements of individual participants. We also made it clear that we would provide feedback only concerning the organizational level, and that we were not acting as experts providing solutions.

Reflections

We were not sure to whom to send the project description: to the contact person, Janice, or the commissioner, Thomas? Normally we would send the contract to the top manager (the commissioner). Why had we been so uncertain about it this time, and in fact chosen a different approach from the one we normally used? We probed our doubts. What could they tell us about the organization? As for the first question, we agreed that it was unclear whether the matter had been delegated. It was interesting that Thomas was actually the one to sign the contract. As for the second question, we became aware that our doubts also reflected our lack of faith that Thomas would participate whole-heartedly in the project. To one of us it had therefore seemed "safer" to send the project description to the highly motivated contact person than to send it to Thomas, lest he "forget" to deal with it. The other one of us, through this soul-searching, uncovered an underlying wish to protect the team and make sure that it would get help. We considered both reactions a danger signal in relation to our neutrality.

Nevertheless, we were pleased and relieved to have the contract back, signed and without comments. At least formally, it was now approved that we could work with a client-system that would be comprehensive enough for us to feel confident about the assignment.

This uncertainty gave rise to the third working hypothesis: *Were we the only ones to be confused about who decided what, or was it a general quality of the management system to generate uncertainty about which level made or was to make a given decision? Was there somehow a connection between this uncertainty and the management's ability to understand and solve problems?*

In our preparations for the meeting, we planned to interview each person in turn, in order to obtain the maximum amount of information, for their benefit as well as ours. It would be especially important to us to interview Paul, whom we had not yet met, about his understanding of the problem and his assessment of the likelihood that things might change.

We were also anxious to see whether a decision had been reached concerning who would be the new team leader. Janice had applied, and by the time of the meeting it might have been decided who would fill the position.

Stage 2: *Interview with three levels of management*

We were anxious to see whether Paul would turn up, since he had not been present at the first meeting. He was there—albeit taciturn and on guard.

At the beginning of the meeting, we were informed that the selection procedure had been completed and that Janice was to be the new team leader. Janice looked pleased.

Most of the meeting took place in a tense atmosphere. It was our impression that it was a rare occasion for the three managers to be together in one room. New aspects of the troublesome past were revealed. The previous team leader, Esther, turned out to have been Paul's brainchild. She was selected despite the team's active resistance. Paul expressed great bitterness with the team and made several derogatory comments about it. Thomas was very understanding about the difficult situation that the team was in, because the employees had not had anywhere to go with their problems and frustrations. "We never lent an ear", as Thomas reflected. When we asked what it might take to move on, Paul recommended that Janice "get tough" with the team. Janice appealed to the other managers for support but got no response from Paul. Thomas, however, declared his willingness to tell the team how he had experienced the events and the aspects had seemed difficult to him. Both the head of department and the head of office expressed their recognition of the team's professional competence. However, they did not feel that the team was utilizing these skills sufficiently, because it was stuck in the past. Thomas said that he was tired of having the past in his face all the time.

The meeting was concluded with a discussion of the next stages in the project and the roles of the managers and the consultants, respectively.

Reflections

After the meeting, we wondered about Paul's position and role. He had held a managerial position in the department for years and seemed—to us—defeatist and bitter. A year and a half prior to our involvement there had been a major reorganization of the department. Paul had been assigned a new position in this structure, and it was at this time that the previous team leader had been hired.

It was one thing for the team leader to feel that Paul was against them because he had supported the previous team leader. But was that sufficient explanation as to why he appeared to be so completely out of the loop in the current system of management? We could not gauge this but figured that we probably did not need to. Whatever the reason, at some point in time a *vicious spiral may have developed at the organizational level*. This, then, was our fourth working hypothesis, which we pictured as shown in Figure 4.3.

Perhaps this vicious spiral had exacerbated the problems and also led to a sense among the persons involved that it was difficult to escape on one's own. This working hypothesis was an important step towards developing a circular understanding of the problems

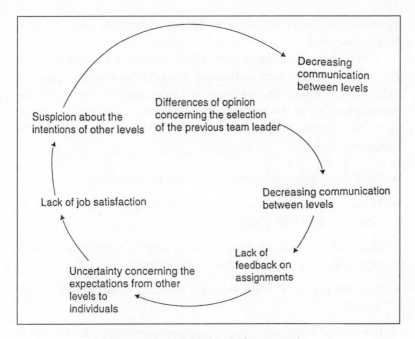

FIGURE **4.3.   Vicious spiral concerning
the communication between levels**

(see p. 107). Helped by the working hypothesis, we began to plan
the half-day seminar with the team, including Janice.

Stage 3. *Half-day seminar with the team*

We had three hours at our disposal. We opened the working seminar by expressing our understanding for the difficult past that was
still present in the team in the form of questions about what had
really happened, doubts, and uncertainties. We suggested that the
time be spent examining the part of the past that continued to be
around today, upsetting the work process. We encouraged everybody to contribute with aspects and versions of the story. The
team was then divided into randomly selected pairs, and each
person was asked to interview the partner about his or her
questions, doubts, and uncertainties about past events. All the

contributions were written on the flip-chart and grouped into three categories.

After mutual briefing, they were divided into new groups, based on their functions within the team. These new groups were asked to work with the findings and to choose the two most important themes to discuss within the framework of this consultation. The themes touched on both the past and the future, with questions such as:

• Why did it take management so long to intervene?

• What could we have done to prevent things from getting out of hand the way they did?

• How can we change the general feeling of suspicion towards and lack of confidence in the management?

• Can we expect a more trusting working environment in the future?

• How should cooperation with management be conducted in the future?

The seminar was concluded with a round concerning how we might move on from here. The one-day seminar was a week away.

Reflections

We were quite pleased with the seminar—first of all, because we had managed to create more flexibility in the individual team members' thinking, as it had been made clear that they were not dealing with one history, but with many different perceptions and interpretations of events; and, secondly, the team had become more curious about management's experience of the whole affair. The participants had also become more interested in discovering how the past might be used for learning something that could help build the future.

One way that the differences in perception was apparent was in a division between the "old-timers", who seemed more dispirited and pessimistic, and the "newcomers", who seemed impatient to move on.

We also noticed that many team members were focusing on the importance of communication as a means for moving on, at the same time as there seemed to be the assumption that good communication was possible only in the presence of personal sympathy. So, if there was antipathy between two persons, it was assumed that communication would necessarily be impaired.

Our fifth working hypothesis, therefore, had to do with the assumptions in the team; we wondered *whether values, such as respect for the individual, caring and close personal relations, had come to be so prominent that it was difficult to keep function and person separate?* On this basis, we decided to begin the one-day seminar with a positive reframing of the problems, which we would describe in terms of organizational dilemmas. Our idea was that if we could shift the focus from the personal level (with blame, guilt, and shame) to the organizational, we would be able to expand the scope of understanding, thus creating better conditions for progress.

The hypothesis about the vicious spiral (Figure 4.3) led to the idea of working with communication tools. We therefore decided to provide explicit instruction in constructive communication, on the basis of a model from the area of assertion training (Dickson, 1982). We were aware that time was running out. Something had to happen quickly. We hoped that instruction (a form of intervention that we otherwise rarely use) at this time would succeed in giving the client-system energy and new positive experiences with successful communication.

Stage 4: *One-day seminar with the whole team*

We began by asking permission to provide feedback describing our assessments of the situation. From our vantage point as consultants, we would "think out loud" about our hypotheses. The team was very interested in hearing our thoughts. We then worked as a reflecting team, formulating different angles to reaching an understanding of the organization. This part took 30 minutes and had the following content:

- Praise for the team for its robustness: it had survived and managed to get help.

- A hypothesis that the difficulties might be understood as conflicts between two cultures: a role-based culture, in which the ground rules of the formal system apply to problem solving, and a task-based culture with completely different rules; we described these two cultures in more detail.

- A hypothesis that while there was great clarity concerning the professional aspects of the roles as manager and employee, great uncertainty surrounded the relationship between the staff members as well as that aspect of the management role that dealt with human resources management; unclear roles could impair the communication.

- A sense that the organization—despite its emphasis on communication—lacked the tools for constructive communication between the organizational levels.

During our presentation, it would have been possible to hear a pin drop. We then asked the team to reflect on our observations in pairs, based on the question: what does this make you think? In the ensuing process, the participants were very thoughtful and very open to each other's considerations.

We then gave an outline of our plans for the day: first, a focus on communication tools, then the planning of the coming dialogue with management.

This proposal resulted in the team splitting into two. The "old-timers" declared that, although they saw the sense in our suggestion, things were now moving much too fast. They had so much pent-up bitterness that they could not keep up. They were also afraid that if they did not get some things off their chest, they might "blow up" in an inappropriate way at the meeting with the management. The "newcomers" thought it was fine to move along as we had suggested. We did a round to find out what the individual participants needed. It became clear that the very different needs of the two sub-groups could not be accommodated within the same process and at the same speed—at least, we did not see how. We therefore suggested an improvised session for the "old-timers" on one of the following days, dedicated exclusively to working with their troublesome emotions.

This proposal was very well received. It made it possible for the "old-timers" to participate in the events planned for the rest of the day.

After lunch, we worked with communication, and individual participants were given the opportunity of assessing their preferred modes of communication from the point of view of an assertion model. Later, smaller groups would draft suggestions for actual questions to be presented in writing to the head of department and the head of office before the concluding seminar. Each question was subjected to critical sparring from the other members concerning whether it had been framed in an assertive way. Janice would bring the questions to the head of department and to the head of office, so that they would have time to prepare.

Reflections

During the one-day seminar, the extent of the perceived distance between the team and both the head of department and the head of office became increasingly clear to us. We based this impression on the persistent questions from the team about the managers' actions, considerations, and reasoning. Many team members had difficulties seeing that there even were any. It also became clear to us that we had become very close with the team and very good at empathizing with their difficulties. We felt great sympathy with the team—so much so that we had even offered to conduct an additional consultation (free of charge) for the "old-timers". We were genuinely concerned about how the current developments looked from Thomas's and Paul's positions, and whether we had jeopardized our freedom of movement. Were we turning our alliance with the team into a coalition against the management?

According to the original project description, the next step was the seminar with both the team and the management. However, we no longer felt that this was an appropriate way to proceed.

The day on which the one-day seminar had taken place we

therefore decided to write a letter to Thomas, suggesting an additional meeting with the two managers. This meeting was to have two purposes:

1. to bring management up to speed with the team by giving them the opportunity to hear the same feedback that we had given the team;

2. to provide counselling concerning their participation in the seminar.

We made it clear that this proposal entailed an additional fee.

Stage 5: *Meeting with the management*

We were informed over the telephone that the meeting was ok, and a date was set at very short notice. At the meeting, the head of department, the head of office, and the team leader were present. In the meantime, the team leader had presented the team's questions to the management. Our observations concerning the organizational dilemmas met with great interest, especially from Thomas. We sensed a certain relief on his part that we were focusing on organizational culture rather than on managerial responsibility.

Paul's reaction to the team's questions was: "They are way out of line here." Janice explained that establishing an open dialogue and greater trust between the team and the management were essential to her chances of being successful in her new position.

At this point, we presented our ideas about how the concluding seminar should be conducted, the distribution of roles, and the ground rules for communication.

It was agreed that both the head of department and the head of office would make a statement early in the seminar, relating their experiences of the course of events.

It was emphasized that these statements needed to include some answers to the team's questions.

Stage 6: *Improvised session with the "old-timers"*

The improvised session had been presented as an open offer to those persons in the team who felt a need for getting some things off their chest. The meeting took place in my office, unlike the other meetings and seminars, which had taken place at the municipality's offices. Four persons accepted the offer. A fifth person had wanted to participate but was unable to make it at such short notice. We carried out two visualization sessions, based on worst-case scenarios from the difficult past. It turned out that the previous team leader, Paul, and Thomas were included in all the imagined situations. The troublesome emotions had to do with feelings of impotence, of letting other people down and being let down, of helplessness, of not being valued, of feeling anger without being able to let it out and guilt towards the previous team leader, who was no longer working in the municipality.

To some, this was the first time they had expressed their feelings—to others. The four participants expressed great relief when the session was over.

Reflections

As the project progressed, we had gained more and more information about interactions between organizational levels—information that shed new light on the hypothesis of the vicious spiral in Figure 4.3. These interactions had consisted of informal meetings between individuals from the team and Thomas (as well as managers in other places in the municipality). This made us wonder about the team's share in maintaining the problem—which led to a new working hypothesis concerning *whether the team's use of informal contacts had contributed to weakening the formal system (that is, the straightforward chain of command from the team to Paul and from Paul to Thomas)?* If this was the case, it might have complicated the problem solving in a situation involving a personal case. Personal cases, where dismissal is a possibility, can in my experience only be handled within the formal system. This would also be the appropriate approach from an ethical point of view.

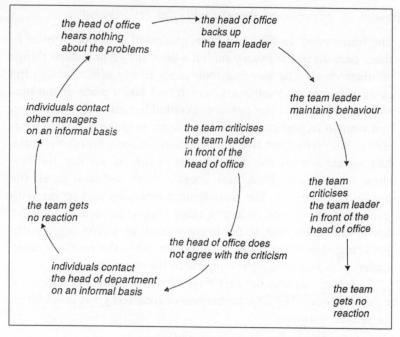

FIGURE **4.4. Vicious spiral concerning the formal
and the informal system**

Perhaps there was a vicious spiral that looked like the one shown in Figure 4.4.

Understanding this spiral made certain things clearer to us. But when planning the concluding seminar, we still had our doubts. We had many ideas, but we did not feel that any of them was really appropriate. In order to progress, we had to air our own worst-case scenarios. One of us feared mostly that Paul's statement would be embarrassing to himself and distressing to the team. The other feared mostly that the whole thing might blow up in our faces. We were afraid that we might have to leave the system after having only made matters worse. Briefly put, we had a problem of our own, which we needed to address first. In a situation like this, it is good to be two consultants working together, because we can test ideas and interview each other. What could we learn from our own reactions?

We became aware that our concerns were blocking our ability to consider how we might help everybody carry out this balancing act, so that they could change their perceptions without losing face.

We also had to look at our own ambitions and ask what it would be realistic to expect from a four-hour seminar. Were we assuming too much responsibility for the situation and slipping out of our roles as consultants? Based on these reflections, we decided to be very careful with the seminar design, making sure that we provided a safety net via the structure and made the participants aware of their options and the fact that they were responsible for making their own choices. The challenge was how to create a room for reflection where all parties participated (see p. 119).

Stage 7: *Concluding seminar with the team and the management*

We opened the seminar by repeating the team's questions and outlining the ground rules for communication and then gave Thomas the floor.

Before the seminar, we had arranged the furniture in such a way that the physical position of the participants reflected their organizational position. The head of department and the head of office sat together at a separate table, the team management, consisting of team leader and chief secretarial assistant, at another separate table, and the function groups within the team at separate tables.

Thomas made a long, well-prepared, open, and very reflective statement about the difficulties that he had experienced during the 13 months. Paul made a brief statement about considerations and decisions.

The sub-groups were then requested to ask additional questions. The participants' reactions revealed that there had been many surprises and new pieces of information in the two statements.

Then followed a dialogue—directed by us—with questions and answers regarding first the past and then the future.

After a break, we outlined the paths that the organization might choose. These paths were based on an expansion of the previous feedback and a presentation of the fourth working hypothesis, about the "vicious spiral", which had until then only existed in our minds. We presented it as our "thinking out loud" and did not invite discussion.

Instead, we asked the participants to reflect in smaller groups on the question: What has made the biggest impression on you today? The round revealed that many participants had learned a great deal about the different experiences of others, and that there was a higher degree of optimism concerning the future cooperation between the organizational levels.

The seminar was concluded by Thomas, who summarized the events of the day. Everybody then gave an individual, written evaluation of the entire consultation.

The evaluations were anonymous but stated the respondent's organizational function. We collected the evaluations and later sent a summary of the evaluations to Janice.

Final evaluation by the participants

In the evaluations, everybody claimed to be "very satisfied" or "satisfied" with the consultation, apart from one person who was "partially satisfied".

The head of department and the head of office were "very satisfied" and "satisfied", respectively. Some typical replies to a question about what the participants had gained were:

- The management's position is clearer to me now.

- I feel that I have a much better understanding of the problems and events before the "solution"/dismissal—also seen from other levels in the organization.

- I have renewed confidence that management actually sees and acts in relation to serious problems. I have a better understanding of the possibilities and constraints at other levels in relation to personal cases.

- We have aired some highly critical emotions.
- We now have insight that makes the events easier to understand.
- The differences have been put into words in a larger forum.
- I feel that I have had a chance to talk the difficult past over in a good and systematic fashion. I have learned to look at the organization in a new way—in positive as well as negative terms.
- I have a greater degree of clarity about the definition of my own function.
- If a situation comes up, I will try to remember the communication model.
- The team is better equipped to handle any problems that may come up.
- I will continue to work on achieving a better dialogue between the team and the management.

Concluding assessment by the consultants

In our assessment, the consultation had had very different meanings to the persons involved, partly based on their position in the organization, partly based on differences in seniority and, thus, their experiences in the administration. For the "old-timers", it had been liberating to get the emotions into the open and put into words. This made them better able to distinguish between old images of persons and the persons as they were today. For the "newcomers", it had been a relief to escape the pressure from the "old-timers" to take over their interpretation of a story that the "newcomers" had not been involved in themselves. The new team leader, who had suffered the mid-level manager's predicament, was in an improved situation now. The taboos had been discussed openly, and there had been direct and indirect attempts at laying down ground-rules for future cooperation within the team and between the various organizational levels.

Thomas had had the opportunity to tell his side of the story and to be listened to, which had not happened before.

Paul's position in the hierarchy had been made more visible.

The management and the social workers' team had a shared language now that they could use in other forms of problem solving.

All in all, we were pleased with our contributions as consultants. Regardless of the degree of satisfaction, however, we have to ask: What could we have done differently and better during this consultation? We had two main concerns: First of all, we were not sure to what extent Paul would be able to live up to his responsibility for human resources management in relation to the team. We were not satisfied with our own achievements in establishing contact with him. His position in the management hierarchy had been made more visible, but did he feel that he had received any help? In retrospect, we felt that we should have worked harder to establish an independent psychological contract with him.

A second concern was that we would have liked to anchor the communication and cooperation more firmly in formal procedures and meeting fora. The concluding seminar ended with ideas for this, but with no actual plans. However, we did not see how we could have accomplished that in the amount of time available to us. We could have solved this problem by re-negotiating the contract and suggesting an additional session. We elected against this, however, since it might send a message to the client-system that, in our opinion, they had not progressed far enough. So we chose to settle with the notion that in this client-system, the participants were basically satisfied and felt that they had received the help they had asked for: to escape the past and face the future.

Turning systemic ideas into practice

In our work on this assignment, we were very much inspired by systemic thinking. In the following, I will discuss those concepts and ideas that we found particularly useful.

There are many versions of reality

It is a basic assumption in systemic thinking that there is no objective reality "out there" that one can perceive and understand with more or less accuracy. Reality is a social construct, created by people who interact and communicate with each other through the means of language. To the consultant, this means that it is always an open question how the members of the organization perceive their individual realities and what processes led to this.

In my work as a consultant—both to large and to small organizations—I have often been amazed (even though I "know") to see how many and how different the existing versions of reality can be and how they influence decisions and actions. One reason that this is possible is, of course, that these versions are usually implicit. Everybody takes his or her own version for granted and assumes that it is shared by many others.

This case study is a good illustration of the way that organizational position and personal experiences in the organization may influence one's version of reality. But other factors play a part too, for example subcultures, profession, power games, and so forth. To the individual, it can be liberating to have a chance to tell one's story in the light of other people's stories. When the past is reinterpreted, new options are created. When—as in this consultation—many members of the organization perceive the problem as a conflict, there is a great risk for communication to become closed. This causes the various versions to remain concealed, which means that they do not enter into the accessible meaning structures where collective learning can take place (see chapter 2).

In the case at hand, this understanding meant that we, as consultants, tried especially hard to find new ways of displaying our interest and curiosity. The attitude underlying our interventions was: "It is going to be interesting to see how different persons describe and explain the difficult past." The assignments and questions that we presented to the participants aimed at encouraging the individual to put his thoughts into words and exchange thoughts and understandings with others.

When, for example, we placed the participants in the room according to their position in the hierarchy, we did this in order to make it easier to see how strongly one's organizational position influenced the context for understanding the problem. (See chapter 1 for a more detailed discussion of the concept of context.)

Focusing on relationships and connections

Systemic thinking employs both a linear causality and a circular understanding of connections (see section 5.2).

In my experience, the linear everyday logic is very common in most organizations. In this consultation, for example, it was expressed in the feeling that "we are the victims of an uninterested and indecisive management". One's own experiences and actions are felt to be the natural reactions to other people's attitudes and intentions. Events are understood and explained piecemeal, in bits that consist of simple links between cause and effect. In addition, there tends to be a strong desire to place the blame somewhere, an image of oneself as a victim, and a development of negative stereotypes, where others are perceived as hostile.

It is a big step to be able to perceive actions and events as created not primarily by persons, but through relations, and to be able to see one's own actions, not just as effects, but also as the "cause" of other people's perception of reality and, thus, a contributing factor to other people's actions.

In this consultation there were many "aha!" experiences for the participants, when they learned how the actions or non-actions of team members had contributed to maintaining the problem. For example, that the negative stereotype of the nearest manager had made some members skip this level and go directly to Thomas. Such actions undermine the formal system, which is, however, the system best suited for handling a personal case.

There are a number of methods and techniques that the consultant can use in order to promote an insight into circular connections. What we did in this case was to begin with tasks that dealt with the contents of the participants' understanding of the problem. It is always important to meet the participants where they are. When dealing with a situation that some feel overwhelmed by, this becomes even more important. Only when the participants feel that they are being understood is it possible to go from content to process. When dealing with the process, it is possible to investigate how and when the "problem" came to be construed as a problem, and how the problem relates to organizational relations and processes (see chapter 1). In the case at hand, we did this through the consultants' reflections and the reframing that we offered at several points.

Dynamic complexity

Focusing on relations and connections constitutes a major shift in perspective. In organizations it is particularly complicated because of the distances in time and space that characterize organizational life. A person's actions in one section of the organization lead to reactions in other sections, but the person has no possibility of observing these and linking them to his own actions. There may also be a significant delay in reactions.

Peter Senge (1990) has given an excellent interpretation of this phenomenon in calling it "dynamic complexity". At the individual level it is often possible to learn from experience, because one gets instant feedback on one's actions. This is especially obvious when one is learning skills, like when a child learns to ride a bicycle: there is instant feedback as to whether or not the bicycle is still in balance and moving forward. Or when the adult attempts to use a foreign language—can he make himself understood or not? Reactions from other people provide instant feedback.

Many—well, probably most—situations in organizations, however, are characterized by the absence of instant feedback. To a member of an organization, it is difficult to link actions together. And to make it even trickier: the meaning-forming processes are usually implicit.

In this previous case study, the fourth working hypothesis illustrates the phenomenon of dynamic complexity. We are dealing here with processes that are created by many different agents at different organizational levels and which increase over time, but of which the individual sees only a small corner. Dialogue across the divisions in the organization is a prerequisite to progress. Creating the conditions for this is one of the consultant's most important tasks.

Establishing room for reflection

When carrying out the daily work with short-term requirements and under time-pressure, it is particularly difficult to notice the connections and processes that take place and change character over time. In processes of change and learning, time is of the essence (see chapter 2).

Over the years, I have heard many managers express their frustration with this. Demands for decisiveness and efficiency do not encourage the use of reflection to explore unknown results, nor do they encourage any discussion about different versions of reality.

Establishing the necessary room for reflection is an important condition for making it possible to recognize long-term processes. In this connection, the theory of the three professional domains is very inspiring (see section 5.4).

In practical consultation work, it is important to find ways of establishing a room that promotes both individual and collective learning.

In this case, where the level of conflict was high and the mutual distrust ran deep, we had to use a great deal of energy thinking about how to create this room. We felt that an important first condition was to keep the "warring factions" separate and to establish a trusting relationship between ourselves and each organizational level. We created this possibility through the project design. The next step was to create tasks as well as a framework for carrying them out that would promote the generation of data, which is the first step in the collective learning process (see chapter 2). In order to make the participants feel safe, we emphasized clear, explicit structures and roles and frequent clarifications of the context.

The extensive body of literature that has been published in recent years about individual and collective learning has been a great source of inspiration to us in this connection.

The consultants become part of the observing system

One of the big steps in the development of systemic thinking was the transition from first-order cybernetics to second-order cybernetics (see section 5.1). In first-order cybernetics, the focus is on the individuals or the organizations as objects that can be described in themselves and independently of the person who is observing and describing them. In second-order cybernetics, it is assumed that the understanding of the object is context-dependent and says as much about the person making the description as it does about the object. In other words, "objective observation" is a contradiction in terms.

In extension of this, it is an important point for me as a consultant that I cannot consider myself a distant, neutral observer. Instead, I become a part of the observing system that surrounds the problem and involved in co-creating new understandings of the problem. My questions and thoughts as a consultant might be different, but they are no more valuable than the questions and thoughts produced by the agents within the client-system. The hypotheses, however—due to the consultant's position outside the organization—may just be different enough to give rise to new meanings and possibilities for action.

In this case study I have described the events with an emphasis on the relationship and the processes that evolved between the client-system and us as consultants. Our thoughts and feelings, which were made clear in this relationship, thus became an important source for learning about the system that was defined by the problem (see chapter 1).

During the consultation there were a number of critical points, where it was beneficial to stop and examine what was happening to ourselves.

In my experience, the more I am able to put myself in a learning position, the better I am able to invite others to do the same. As a consultant, I therefore have to ask myself, for example: "With what thoughts am I meeting the client-system?" or "What would happen, if I replaced thought x with thought y?" The challenge here is simultaneously to show respect for the thoughts that are created by the members of the client-system, and to show irreverence for my own thoughts (see section 5.3 on the concept of irreverence).

CHAPTER FIVE

Key concepts in systemic thinking

Gitte Haslebo & Kit Sanne Nielsen

5.1 *First- and second-order cybernetics*
[Gitte Haslebo]

This chapter focuses on those concepts and basic ideas that we find particularly important for reaching an understanding of systemic thinking. As this is a complex area, it is not easy to select the most important issues. Many writers have contributed to an understanding of the concepts, and the concepts have changed in meaning from the early stages of systemic thinking until today. The greatest shift was the change from first- to second-order cybernetics.

The early stages in organizational psychology were characterized by first-order cybernetics. [Cybernetics is originally a Greek word that means control. Today, cybernetics is the name of the science that deals with the control and regulation of systems (Wiener, 1948).]

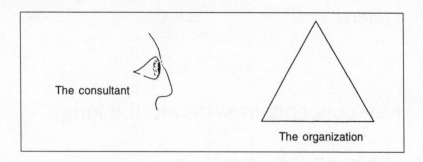

FIGURE 5.1.   First-order cybernetics

First-order cybernetics is based on the assumption that it is possible to understand a system independently of the person who observes it and attempts to describe it. The consultant observes and gathers data about the organization in order to find the qualities that are typical of the organization in question. The organization exists "out there", detached from the consultant. The focus, thus, is on the observed system, as shown in Figure 5.1.

In the figure, the consultant observes the organization and, on the basis of her observations, works out a description of the organization. The description is considered independent of the consultant and of the situations where the observations took place.

The transition to second-order cybernetics was made possible by contributions first from Bateson (1972), Maturana & Varela (1987), von Foerster (1981) and von Glasersfeld (1984) and, later, from the Milan school, whose first work, *Paradox and Counterparadox,* became very influential (Selvini-Palazzoli, Boscolo, Cecchin, & Prata, 1978).

In second-order cybernetics, the focus is not on the observed system but, rather, on the observing system. A system is not considered an objective entity that exists as such, but an image of the world, constructed by people on the basis of their experiences and basic assumptions. In the light of this, we may wonder how we can even have the common experience of speaking to another person about a shared reality. What makes this possible is that we have shared experiences and, thus, have developed common frames of reference. From the perspective of second-order cybernetics, the interesting question, rather, is how we are able to base cognition on experiences. This line of thinking is called constructionist epistemology (epistemology = the study of knowledge). (See, for example, the article by Lynn Hoffman, 1985, about the historical development.)

According to second-order cybernetics, the consultant should consider herself a part of the observing system. The consultant comes to an organization with her personal experiences and theoretical assumptions, and these tint the spectacles through which she looks at the organization. Her understanding of the organization, therefore, is as much a product of her background as of the organization. The challenge for the consultant is to examine how she uses her experiences and concepts to understand the events in the organization—in cooperation with the various parties in the client-system. The consultant can attempt to observe herself as an observer of the organization, but she can never leave herself out of the picture—or, to use a metaphor: she cannot remove her tinted spectacles. (See Figure 5.2.)

To me, an important consequence of this line of thinking is an attempt to remain humble: my understanding of the organization and the problem is only one approach among many—and it may not even be the best approach. It is therefore important to keep an open mind and be open—cognitively—to entertaining alternative approaches.

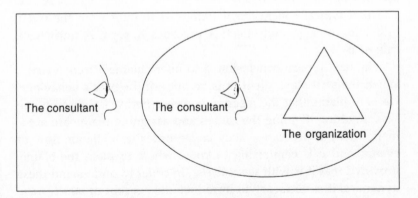

FIGURE 5.2.   Second-order cybernetics

5.2   *The linear and the circular line of thinking*
[Gitte Haslebo]

The linear and the circular line of thinking are two fundamentally different ways of explaining how we know what we know. Our line of thinking determines how we interpret the world around us, what we make of it, how we reach decisions, and how we organize our lives.

In our culture, the linear line of thinking is the most common. When using this approach, we perceive the events that we are part of in fragments—that is, bits of actions that fit together in a certain way. To use an example: in an office meeting, a staff member sees the boss scolding the staff and then sees that her co-workers keep silent. The order of events determines what we perceive as cause and effect. The first event causes the event that follows. That is: the boss's scolding has caused the staff to be silent. (See Figure 5.3.)

The linear line of thinking is common in everyday logic: we attempt to find out what caused the events that we observe, for example in the course of a workday. In the backs of our minds are questions, like: why do the manager, the colleagues, the customers, the users, and so forth, act the way that they do? Not being able to understand other people's actions is perturbing. The same is true of one's own actions. In the linear line of thinking understanding something is the same as identifying the cause. In order to discover the cause, we look for an explanation in the events that transpired immediately prior to the incomprehensible act. The first typical conclusion therefore, is to infer from the order of events to cause and effect: A precedes B, ergo, A must have caused B.

The next typical conclusion is to infer "blame" from "cause". When the staff stays silent, it is because of the boss's behaviour. He is to blame that the meeting becomes boring because no one says anything. Finding the causes and assigning blame are automatic thought processes. They create order in a chaotic flow of events, and it is comforting to know where to place the blame. Provided that it is with *someone else*. In order to understand these dynamics, it is necessary to introduce the concept of *punctuation*. A workday is made up of an endless flow of events. When this

1.		2.
The boss scolds the staff	⇨	The staff stays silent
Cause		Effect

FIGURE 5.3.   Example of the linear approach

flow is divided into fragmented actions, it is the result of a human choice. Not that we consciously choose where in the flow to make the cuts. The "choice" usually takes place in a split-second, as a process that we are unaware of. A number of different factors influence how a particular person is going to *punctuate* the events. In an organization, *position* is a factor with significant influence on the punctuation of events.

To return to the example above, let us attempt to see the meeting as it was perceived by the boss. He has put a number of important issues on the agenda. He needs input from the staff and is annoyed that their contribution is so meagre. His punctuation of the events will be something like Figure 5.4.

The boss sees his actions as a natural response to the silence of the staff members; they are to blame for his behaviour.

The third conclusion in the linear approach is this: if others are to blame for my actions, then they may, in fact, have *intended* for me to act this way. From the staff members' point of view, the situation is exacerbated if they not only see the boss scolding them, but feel that he is doing it in order to shut them up. And, from the boss's point of view, the situation is exacerbated if he not only sees them being silent, but feels that they are being silent in order to spite him and make his job more difficult. Assigning blame is thus often associated with attributing (dubious) motives to the other party.

1.		2.
The staff is not contributing	⇨	I scold them
Cause		Effect

FIGURE 5.4.   Example of the linear approach

1.	2.	3.	4.	5.	6.	7.
The boss ⇨ asks a question	The staff ⇨ members think and stay silent	The boss ⇨ scolds them	The staff ⇨ members think and stay silent	The boss ⇨ asks a question	The staff ⇨ members think and stay silent	The boss scolds them

FIGURE 5.5.   A longer sequence of events

Within the linear approach, an additional conclusion may occur: if others are to blame (and, perhaps, act on the basis of bad intentions), then *they have to be the first to change.* Staff members will feel that only once the boss stops scolding them will they dare speak up. Conversely, the boss will feel that only when the staff members begin to contribute can he stop scolding them.

Linear thinking, thus, often locks thought processes and actions into repetitive patterns that no one can change.

Let us now introduce a third perspective on the events at the office meeting. A visitor is present at the meeting and observes the sequence of events shown in Figure 5.5.

From this longer sequence of events we can see how the boss and the staff members chose different segments. The boss chose Segments 1 through 3, the staff members chose Segments 3 through 4. At the same time, they ignored other segments. The boss does not see the staff members' silence as a reaction to his scolding, and the staff members do not see, for example, that they are not responding to his questions.

Thus, the differences in their punctuation of the events lead not only to different experiences of the office meeting, but also to different interpretations. One common feature in their experiences, however, is that they see themselves as *victims* and the other party as *the culprit.* Another common feature is that by placing the blame with someone else, they relieve themselves of the responsibility for changing the dynamics. Again, it should be pointed out that these dynamics are rarely visible to the parties.

The linear approach, thus, does not promote change. Assigning blame and attributing bad intent is often associated with moral judgement or condemnation. Faced with this, it is a natural reaction for most people to become defensive and to protect their personal integrity. The "culprit" will typically focus his efforts on defending himself, and the "victim" will not even consider changing. They are locked into a pattern with limited options.

An alternative to this approach is the circular line of thinking, which was developed within the framework of second-order cybernetics. In circular thinking, events are seen as parts of a larger pattern. The order of events is of interest, but it does *not* lead to the definition of an act as being either cause or effect. It is mostly a matter of personal preferences whether one wants to say that concepts of "cause" and "effect" are dissolved in circular thinking or that actions and events are seen as *both* cause and effect simultaneously. To avoid connotations of blame, the systemic consultant will usually prefer to talk about *connections* instead of cause and effect. Connections between events can be arranged in circles (which can be perceived as "good circles" or "vicious circles"). It would be more appropriate, however, to talk about spirals, because although the pattern repeats itself, the parties never return to the same point. The events in the office meeting can be construed as a spiral that repeats itself (see Figure 5.6).

In the circular approach, the segmented events and actions should be assembled into a larger whole. The scope is expanded by the inclusion of a longer period of time, additional agents, and feedback mechanisms. It is of interest to see how the various parties' segments fit together. The attention is shifted away from individuals and over to the *pattern* of relations, thoughts, and actions. When the idea about finding *the* cause is abandoned, so, too, is the

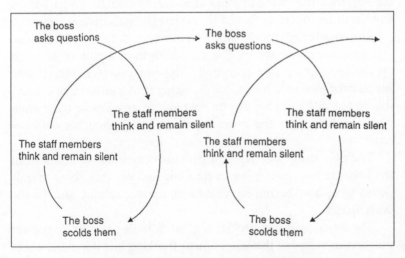

FIGURE 5.6.   **Example of circular thinking**

idea of placing the blame with someone. The moral condemnation is replaced with a curiosity about the complexity of the pattern. Instead of trying to find the culprit(s), it becomes relevant to uncover the part that everybody played in creating and maintaining the pattern of events and actions.

The interest in uncovering (other people's) intentions is supplanted by an interest in examining the *effects*. *Effect* and *intent* are two very different issues. The general communication theory contributed greatly to the shift in focus from intentions to effects (Watzlawik, Bearing, & Jackson, 1967). The important issue is not what the boss intends to say, but what the staff members hear him saying. The question "Why did you do that?" should be replaced with such questions as "What were you hoping to achieve with what you did?" The interesting point is to see what message was received, not what message was sent. Or, in the words of the philosopher Wittgenstein: "I am saying what you are hearing." When patterns of actions become unsatisfactory for the persons involved, it becomes a common project to find out what messages are being *heard*. Back to the office meeting: if it becomes evident that the staff members hear a different message from the one the boss intends to convey, then his only option is to change his communication. And, conversely, if it turns out that the boss hears a different message from the one the staff members are trying to convey, then they have to make changes. In changing a pattern of events, one's first step should be to change one's own actions.

The circular approach, thus, implies very different ideas about change and responsibility. The examination of a pattern is based on the assumption that everybody, to some extent, is responsible for its existence and, hence, for changing it. A pattern like the one illustrated in Figure 5.6 can be changed at any link. Any participant can help alter the general pattern by altering his own behaviour.

The case study in chapter 4 provides examples of shifts from the linear to the circular line of thinking and of ideas about spirals developing and becoming visible to the consultant and to the participants.

The linear and the circular approach both have an important position in systemic thinking. Linear thinking lets the members of an organization supply the necessary building blocks for the circular approach. The consultant working from systemic inspiration has to know and master both approaches and be able to switch between them. Systemic thinking has often been misconstrued as saying that linear thinking is useless and "banned". This, however, is not the case. The reason that the circular approach has attracted so much attention and is often considered more or less identical with systemic thinking is that the linear approach is such a common—and, in many organizations, the only—approach. When management decides to contact a consultant, it is often after a series of failed attempts at solving the given problem through a linear approach. Instead of solving the problem, this has caused the organization to become more and more locked into causal explanations and "the blame game". This is why there is usually a greater need to bring in the circular line of thinking.

The challenge facing the consultant is to show respect for the ways that the members of the organization understand the problem, without getting caught up in determining causal explanations and deciding who gets the blame. When the time is ripe, the consultant should then begin to explore the larger pattern that the problem is embedded in. In order for this to happen, it is essential how the consultant phrases her questions, because some questions encourage a linear line of thinking, others a circular line of thinking. A question like "Why did he say that?" encourages a linear response. Conversely, a question like "What is the difference between office meetings with a great deal of scolding, meetings with only some scolding, and meetings with no scolding at all?" invites a circular response. The circular questioning technique is a general term for types of questions that are well suited for the circular approach. The purpose of circular questioning is to create reflections. It should not be possible to simply answer "yes" or "no". Instead, the circular questions may make the problem owner see the problem from other angles. One way of achieving this is by asking in such a way that the problem owner has to examine his own way of relating to the problem. "When did you first notice signs of this problem?" is an example of a question that encourages an exploration of the process of realization. Thus, the question may help the problem owner detach himself from the problem and put himself in a meta-position to it. When circular questions are asked in an open forum, the consultant's interview of various persons in sequence will promote individual and shared reflections, which helps new interpretations to develop. Questions of "blame", which belong in the linear line of thinking, are replaced with alternative explorations of *meaning*.

How circular questions are created and phrased is a whole separate issue. A discussion of the numerous different types of circular questions would go beyond the scope of this book, but the interested reader may turn to, especially, Karl Tomm (1984) and Tom Andersen (1990).

5.3   *From neutrality to irreverence*
              [Gitte Haslebo]

Neutrality is a key concept in systemic thinking. It is also a concept that has been discussed, criticized, and revised several times. I will first describe the historical development of the concept within family therapy and then its application in organizational consultation.

In 1980, the article "Hypothesizing—Circularity—Neutrality: Three Guidelines for the Conductor of Sessions" (Selvini-Palazzoli, Boscolo, Cecchin, & Prata, 1980) was published. It later proved to be a classic in the field. The reasoning in the article is based on the Milan group's family therapy work.

The article explains two important aspects of the concept of neutrality. First, that neutrality has to do with the therapist's way of relating to the family members. The aim is to make sure that the family feels the therapist to be *impartial*—that is, that she is not siding with any one person more than with anyone else. This is more easily said than done. As it is also pointed out, it is impossible for the therapist to devote an equal amount of attention to everyone *at the same time*. The person to whom the therapist—via her questions—devotes the most attention is going to consider the therapist his ally. Neutrality, therefore, has to be viewed in the light of the time factor. In a key point, neutrality is defined as *the effect that the therapist's overall behaviour has on the family over time*. The therapist has to shift her attention from person to person to create successive alliances that cannot be construed by the family as the therapist choosing sides.

The second meaning of neutrality has to do with the *absence of personal moral evaluations and judgement* of any kind. Comments of evaluation or judgement are going to be perceived by the family members as invitations to form or join alliances or coalitions. If a coalition were to arise, the therapist's distance to one person or subgroup in the family would decrease, while the distance to other persons or subgroups would increase. This would compromise the therapist's meta-position—and, with it, her cognitive flexibility.

The interesting point in this article—which the authors do not make explicitly clear—is that neutrality is not described as a quality in the therapist's personality or actions, but as *an effect on the family*. In other words, neutral is not something that one "is" or "does", but the *perceived effect* of one's actions.

In 1979, the Milan group split up. Selvini-Palazzoli and Prata continued into research, developing new interventions, while Cecchin and Boscolo continued to work with teaching, supervision, and consultation.

One of the results of Selvini-Palazzoli's interest in research was the establishing of a cooperation with a group of students who were all working professionally as psychologists in organizations (companies, hospitals, research centres, and schools). The purpose was to study human behaviour in large organizations. The results of the group's work were published (in Italian in 1981, in English in 1987) in the book *The Hidden Games of Organizations* (Selvini-Palazzoli, 1987). In the 1970s there was little experience with applying systemic concepts to psychological consultations in organizations. The group's many discussions were based on the participants' actual work in the various organizations. In many instances, the psychologist started off on the wrong foot, in the sense that a clear formal and psychological contract had not been drawn up to define the psychologist's relationship with the organization.

It is a fascinating book, consisting of four case studies and a series of theoretical chapters. The case studies describe how the psychologist gets caught up in internal games and power struggles that have been established long before the psychologist becomes involved, and which the psychologist often recognizes too late. The book paints a vivid picture of the complexity of the communication that takes place on three levels in the form of hidden agendas and implicit and explicit appeals to the consultant for help. The difficulties in not getting roped into hidden alliances and coalitions and, thus, choosing sides are made very clear.

The book does not provide a comprehensive, explicit treatment of these difficulties in relation to the concept of neutrality. Implicitly, however, neutrality is understood as the art of remaining impartial in the complex world of large organizations.

Some of the concepts and techniques that one can employ in order to maintain neutrality, however, are introduced here.

The Milan group's first interpretation of the concept of neutrality (from 1980) was the object of much debate and criticism. The critics felt that neutrality would create a therapist who was uninterested and cold, who lacked distinct opinions, and who would not accept any responsibility when faced with immoral acts. Among the critics were the feminists, who felt that this neutrality would mean an acceptance of the oppression of women and who therefore felt that neutrality was essentially unethical.

In 1987, Cecchin therefore felt put upon to address the issue of neutrality again which he did in the article "Hypothesizing, Circularity, and Neutrality Revisited: An Invitation to Curiosity" (Cecchin, 1987). In the article, he emphasizes that neutrality should be understood as *the creation of curiosity* and as *an obligation to develop different approaches*. Curiosity is not to be used in a search for the best description or explanation of the family's problem but, rather, to focus on patterns and ponder how all these family members' (different) descriptions fit together. Cecchin calls this interest in patterns an *aesthetic* interest that feeds curiosity and respect. Respect is a prerequisite for curiosity. We have closed conclusions regarding people for whom we have no respect in our everyday lives ("He is *completely* incompetent", "They are *absolutely* impossible to work with"). Closed conclusions do not promote curiosity. In this sense, the respect for other people becomes a prerequisite for the ability to remain curious about them. The aesthetic interest enables the person to rise cognitively to a meta-level, which offers a better opportunity for getting a comprehensive view of the statements of several people. Thus, there are three ingredients to neutrality: curiosity, aesthetic interest, and respect.

Neutrality is a challenge for the therapist—a challenge that it can be hard to live up to. Cecchin therefore also discusses how the therapist can become aware that she is about to compromise her neutrality. He mentions two sets of symptoms: psychosomatic symptoms and boredom. The therapist should be aware what type of psychosomatic symptoms she is most likely to develop (for example, headaches or stomach pains).

Boredom occurs when there is no information that makes a difference to the therapist. This may happen when the therapist "becomes engaged to her hypotheses". The circular interview (see section 5.2) and the formation of hypotheses (see section 5.5) involve techniques that the therapist can employ in order to break off her "engagement".

In 1992, there was a new contribution to the understanding of neutrality, with a title that may at first glance seem a bit funny: *Irreverence: A Strategy for Therapists' Survival* (Cecchin, Lane, & Ray, 1992).

The book is based on experiences from a number of contexts where Cecchin had worked as a supervisor or consultant to professional therapists dealing with extremely difficult cases (violence, incest, rape, suicidal tendencies, and so forth).

The authors describe how they arrived at the belief that *the irreverent* position might be a strategy for survival in these severe cases. After having suffered, for years, from doubts about what they should do in the face of these cases, the authors concluded that this doubt should be considered an asset.

Irreverence here means the courage to question critically *one's own ideas as a therapist and consultant,* combined with respect for the persons with whom one works. Essentially, the lack of irreverence towards one's own ideas is an irresponsible position, because it may make a person blind to the potentially unethical consequences of her own actions. This does not mean that one should meet a client-system without any ideas, theories, or hypotheses. On the contrary—the authors claim that it requires thorough knowledge of theories and ideas to be able to face them with irreverence and doubt.

The therapist should meet the client-system with hypotheses and respect—*and* with curiosity and the willingness to replace proposed hypotheses with others that might prove more useful. In order to accomplish this, the therapist has to be able to reflect on the consequences of her own attitudes, basic assumptions, and actions.

In this historical development one can see the contours of the transition from first- to second-order cybernetics. Neutrality, in the sense of impartiality, is a concept that belongs to first-order cybernetics. The focus is on the client-system and the effect that the therapist's actions have on the client-system. Neutrality in the sense of curiosity is a very broad concept that can be understood within both first- and second-order cybernetics.

Neutrality in the sense of impartiality and curiosity were (and are) important concepts that can help the therapist and consultant to distinguish their activities from expert advice. The expert's job is to place his expertise at the commissioner's disposal. In doing so, the expert enters into a long-term relationship with the commissioner—an alliance that may turn into coalitions with others. The expert advisor deals with the contents aspect of the commissioner's problems and works within a framework of linear thinking.

With the development of the ideas about the circular line of thinking and the transition to second-order cybernetics, the neutrality concepts, however, proved insufficient. There was a need for a concept that could help the therapist and the consultant act as part of the observing system. This is where the concept of *irreverence* enters into the picture. The focus shifts from the client-system to the point where the consultant's theoretical assumptions, attitudes, and experiences direct her learning about the client-system and about the relationship between herself and the client-system. It then becomes interesting to ponder the following question: "I wonder what the client-system would look like if I met it with other ideas?"

To me, both neutrality and irreverence are indispensable concepts to the organizational consultant. Not that the concept of irreverence replaces the concept of neutrality. In my experience, actual consultations hold plenty of invitations that—if I were to accept them—would compromise my impartiality as a consultant.

The invitations can be about choosing sides in a conflict, determining who is right, joining secret groups or meetings, participating in the moral condemnation of a manager, expressing my take on the core of the problem, recommending a particular solution, and so forth. Such direct or indirect invitations can be seen as thoughts and actions within the linear approach. In the given situation, I, as the consultant, have to choose whether I want to continue my inquiry within a linear framework, or whether I want to switch to the circular approach. In this situation, it is important to carry on both an internal and an external dialogue. In the internal dialogue I focus on my own thoughts, emotions, and personal judgement. On the basis of my professional identity, I will censor this dialogue and select the elements that will be the most useful in the external dialogue. To maintain a meta-position the consultant, in effect, has to have a dual consciousness.

Chapters 6 and 7, which are about the consultant's cognitive processes in practice, describe how supervision and cooperation with another consultant can be employed as a means of helping the consultant maintain her neutrality and increase her irreverence towards her own thoughts and ideas.

This section may give the reader the impression that the systemically inspired consultant *always* has to try to stay neutral. This is not the case, however. This question is the subject of the following section, about professional domains.

5.4   *The professional domains*
                    [Gitte Haslebo]

Since Cecchin's article in 1987, many other systemically inspired therapists and consultants have continued to develop the concept of neutrality—as, for example, Lang, Little, and Cronen in their article "The Systemic Professional Domains of Action and the Question of Neutrality" (1990).

This is a very inspiring (but rather inaccessible) article, where the authors set out to develop the understanding of the concept of neutrality in relation to the criticism that had been levied against it. The point of departure for the article is the inherent conflict in the systemic consultant's condition: on the one hand, she has to stay neutral towards the client's development efforts and, on the other, she will encounter situations that require her to take a stand. Therapists rarely have a job situation that allows them to work exclusively as therapists; part of the time they will have to act as social supervisors, overseeing various rules and regulations.

How should this conflict between roles and tasks be managed and understood? This is where the domain theory comes in. It was Maturana who introduced the concept of the *domain* in 1985 (in an unpublished paper) and provided the background for it in the famous book, *The Tree of Knowledge* (Maturana & Varela, 1987).

Domain refers to a space for professional activities that is defined in time. The authors' aim with the article is to suggest how one can distinguish between various types of activities that professionals carry out, while adhering to the basic ideas in systemic thinking. A fundamental concept is Maturana's understanding that human language acts unfold in three different domains: the domains of ethics, production, and explanations, respectively. The three authors mentioned above especially use examples from the area of social work, treatment, and therapy. In the following I present the ideas from the article, expanded with examples from organizational consultation. I refer to the domain of explanations as the domain of *reflection*, as this concept, in my opinion, better expresses the key aspects of this domain.

The three domains can be understood as three basic types of contexts (see chapter 2). In a given situation, all three domains exist simultaneously, but since it is impossible to employ three different frames of reference at the same time, one of them is going to assume the foreground and control the events.

In the *domain of aesthetics*, ideas and values such as beauty, harmony, accordance, desirability, morals, and ethics are predominant. Any situation has an ethical dimension, but not all situations require professional attention to ethical questions. When they do, it is often expressed in intense, unpleasant, or even painful considerations for the professional. For example, it may turn out, at the beginning of a leadership seminar, that the psychological contract between top management and the participants—

counter to the consultant's assumption—has not been discussed thoroughly enough. The participants feel that they are in a coercive situation. The consultant knows that learning only rarely takes place in coercive situations. When the consultant becomes aware of the participants' perception of the situation, the consultant's context changes and the aesthetic domain becomes dominant. The ethical dilemma before the consultant raises unpleasant questions, such as: Should I cancel the course? Should I carry on with the course—perhaps just to pass the time? Can a dialogue be established between top management and the participants? Should the consultant's contract with top management be annulled or renegotiated?

In the domain of aesthetics, the consultant *cannot* remain neutral. In this domain, the consultant is forced to consider how theory, practice, and ethics are connected—or, rather, not connected. This is an essential part of one's professional training: acquiring the ability to consider the ethical consequences of the way that one makes theory, methods, and techniques interact.

The domain of aesthetics is considered superior to the domains of both production and reflection. The choice of understanding one's work within either the domain of production or the domain of reflection is governed by considerations taking place in the domain of aesthetics. If the consultant is unsure about this choice, she has to revert to the domain of aesthetics.

In extension of these points, systemic consultation should be understood as a practice that springs from an ethical position. Ethical issues can always be traced back to considerations concerning the extent to which *the given practice is going to contribute to increasing the future possibilities for change, development, and growth.*

In the *domain of production,* reality is considered objective: there is one truth, and it is this truth that it is essential to uncover. The idea of one universe is predominant. Practice in the domain of production springs from well-defined technologies based on conventions that are widely accepted. The criteria for good versus inferior work are well known and accepted. The assessment of persons by, for example, social workers, diagnoses by doctors, psychological tests by psychologists, and arbitration by lawyers in conflicts about collective agreements are all examples of professional practice based on well-established knowledge, known methods, and careful procedures. They are, thus, examples of activities within the domain of production.

This does not necessarily mean that it is easy for the professional to function within the domain of production, because she can "simply" stick to conventions. Often, it is not that simple. Experts, too, may disagree as to what is the best technology, just as there may be great variation in what the professionals, on the one side, and the company, on the other, consider the success criteria for the execution of a given task. The nature of these differences is brilliantly described in, for example, the book *The Clash of Cultures: Managers and Professionals* (Raelin, 1985).

The domain of production employs linear thinking as well as cause-and-effect thinking (see section 5.2). In this line of thinking, events are considered the effects of distinct causes: the sales staff is not thriving *because* the manager is no good at human resources management. The cause can be found in the manager's (poor) skills at human resources management, and the effect is low job satisfaction for the staff. This understanding is based on the underlying assumption that the parties in an interaction are separate entities that are not connected to each other as parts of a system. The interaction is uni-directional and sequentially ordered: first comes the cause, then the effect.

Within the domain of production, clarity is held in high regard, and an either/or approach is typical. This affects consultations that take place within the domain of production. In the case of the conflict about the correct interpretation of the collective agreement, the question to the lawyer is: who is right, the shop steward or management? Other examples include questions to the consultant, such as: is there too much wasted time in the work procedure (yes or no)? Is the low degree of job satisfaction in the sales department due to poor management (yes or no)?

Consultation within the domain of production is often supposed to lead to the identification of the factors that caused the problems. Going back to the questions above, the task may be to find out why the procedures are inefficient or the main reasons for the poor working environment. Finding the causes is often associated with placing the blame. When the consultant makes recommendations based on her findings, she explicitly takes a stand on the nature and course of the changes—and, in that sense, is not neutral.

Professional work in the domain of production often has the character of reaching a conclusion, so that management can make a decision. The consultant will, therefore, typically not be considered neutral, in the sense of being impartial. If, for example, the consultant finds the cause of the poor working environment really to *be* poor management, the manager is not likely to consider the consultant neutral. I refer here to the previous discussion about the concept of neutrality (see section 5.3), where the key criterion for neutrality lay in the client-system's perception of what the consultant does (and not in the consultant's self-image or intentions).

The expert advisor, by definition, cannot be impartial. It is, however, important that the aspect of neutrality that deals with *curiosity* is also a guide for the consultant's work in the domain of production. An assessment of a manager, for example, should be carried out on the basis of a genuine curiosity about the new data. Professional work means that the result is not known ahead of time and is not controlled, for example, by leading questions. It is also a quality requirement that the assessment take place with the client's consent. This is not always possible, however. For example, a social worker may have to carry out a judgement when parents are suspected of neglecting or abusing a child. As a minimum requirement, the parents should be informed about the background for the investigation and about their options. To the external organizational consultant, the consent of the participants in, for example, a course or an investigation is essential, since, frequently, the formal contract will have been negotiated only with a few people in top management. This necessitates a possibility for establishing a psychological contract with the people who are going to participate in the course or investigation. Sometimes the practical possibilities for this are not present or satisfactory. There may not be time, for example, or the consultant may not be permitted to meet with the participants prior to the beginning of the project. (See also the section in chapter 2 on defining the participant group.)

In *the domain of reflection*, reality is considered a subjective construct: there are many experiences, perceptions, and explanations.

This domain has a *multi*verse, meaning that there is a multiplicity of stories and perspectives, which are of equal rank. The work of the professional is governed by neutrality, seen as impartiality, curiosity, and irreverence towards the consultant's own ideas— still subject to the ethical requirement of increasing the potential for development and growth.

The domain of reflection employs the circular approach. It is important to examine how each person's thoughts, emotions, and actions influence and are influenced by those of other people, and how they fit into the larger pattern within the system. Depending on the way that the various members of the organization punctuate the events, any action can be construed both as "cause" and "effect". Not only is it impossible to know which came first, the chicken or the egg, reaching such a conclusion is also irrelevant. The important issue is to examine and convey how the various positions in the organization contribute to labelling some relations and connections as important and others as unimportant—and to the different meanings attributed to them.

In the domain of reflection, every story is of equal validity and is considered important input for the common dialogue. The consultant's attitude is to be curious about and interested in the stories. It is her job to be an "explorer, map maker, story elaborator and co-creator" (Lang et al., 1990).

Neutrality also requires the consultant to keep an open and inquisitive mind to possible changes and their direction and speed. It is the client-system that makes the choices and decisions.

After this discussion of domain theory, I discuss how domains are connected to the typology of consultancy approaches that was established in chapter 1.

As it will probably be evident from the previous section, expertise consultation is a form of consultation best understood as a professional practice in the domain of production. It employs the notion of an objective reality, of which the expert is able to provide more concise description and analysis than the organization itself is capable of. Answers and solutions to problems can be closer to or farther from the truth. Expertise consultation would bring them closer to the truth. Expertise consultation, thus, is based on a certain theory of cognition, the positivist approach.

Systemic thinking has made many and valuable contributions to the development of methodology within the domain of reflection. This development is anchored in general communication theory and the theory of social constructionism, which states that reality is co-constructed in a dialogue between individuals.

Now, it might appear tempting to equate systemic consultation with consultation in the domain of reflection, but this would be incorrect. However, the domain theory is a good aid for helping the systemically inspired consultant take in the situation and make sensible choices. It is one of the consultant's tasks to consider the domains and create movements between them. Even if a consultation assignment is defined as lying within the domain of reflection, it may be fruitful to shift the activity to the domain of production. This can be done during the process, for example if a group of participants is blocking, because a management decision is required. A shift to the domain of production should always happen by the end of a consultation. It is important that the participants assume responsibility and take charge of the process of converting the insight that was reached in the domain of reflection to decisions and action plans.

One of the implications of this is that the key success criteria and quality requirements for a given consultation depend on the domain where the consultation is to be understood.

In consultations within the domain of production, the most valued elements are objectivity and concise data processing. A criterion for good quality in expert advice, for example, is that the consultant attempt to leave her own personality out of the analysis, to prevent the findings from being biased by her personal values (and prejudices).

The success criteria and quality requirements in the domain of reflection stem from the ethical requirement, which is an element in systemic thinking, namely—as I have mentioned before—that *the given practice contribute to increasing the possibilities for future change, development, and growth.*

At this point, the interesting question is: can expert advice lead to change? When, for example, managers and staff are placed in a new structure, this is a change in the way the formal side of the organization and the people in the organization are combined. But that does not necessarily constitute change, if this is to be understood as changes and development in people's thoughts, emotions, and behaviour. It is a change that comes from the outside, not from the inside (see also chapter 2). According to the domain theory, consultation in the domain of production is not capable of promoting human development, but only of promoting conclusions and decisions.

We may conclude, therefore, that if the goal is to attain organizational development as a product of human development, then professional considerations about links between theory, method, and ethics show that the consultation should be carried out primarily in the domain of reflection.

Problems like "the organization is not thriving" or "poor cooperation" or "management incompetence" are best handled through methods in the domain of reflection, where there is room for differing experiences and mental models and a focus on interpersonal relationships rather than on the individual. When this happens, thoughts can move freely and there is room for increased communication, both of which are prerequisites to development.

One of the key issues in the initial contract phase, therefore, is to open a discussion and secure a shared understanding as to whether the particular consultation is best solved within the domain of production or reflection. Since the consultant will often negotiate with people from different organizational levels—level by level—there is a real risk of different understandings of this. If top management perceives a consultation as expertise consultation while the staff sees it as the beginning of a process for improving cooperation and relations, and the manager in charge is not sure what is going on, then this *lack of clarity about the context* alone will be an additional source of conflict rather than a contribution to solving the problem.

5.5   *Hypothesizing*
                         [Kit Sanne Nielsen]

Organizations are in constant development, because natural evo-
lution is inherent in organizational processes. Constant change
means inevitable conflicts among the members of the organization. Specific conflict-solving techniques are needed for solving
these controversies. In systemic thinking, hypotheses are considered an effective means for creating change, for example by including observed actions. Let us assume that a human resources
function initiates a management development programme. This
causes strong reactions in the target group in the form of suspicion
towards top management. "What are they up to now—aren't we
doing our job well enough?" In this situation, the systemic consultant can form a hypothesis that sheds light on this unspoken
suspicion. The hypothesis describes how the actions of the human
resources consultants appear to meet with severe scepticism or
massive criticism. In this way the hypothesis, when shared with
the client-system, also functions as an intervention. If the hypothesis is accepted, the target group has gained an insight, which
may prevent similar reactions to future initiatives.

The hypothesis is *feedback* on certain reactions as well as an
attempt to understand a specific interaction. But the hypothesis
also raises new and probing questions, for example in the case
described above: "What is the hypothesis going to mean for management's relations with the participants in the future?"

The word "hypothesis" originally comes from the Greek and
means: a scientific statement that "lies under". Here, we use a
hypothesis about a statement that expresses what goes on between
the lines in a particular context. This means that it is a constructed
picture of connections between experiences.

In systemic consultation, the hypothesis is one of the consultant's *key tools*. By hypothesizing, the consultant shines a temporary spotlight on certain conditions.

Systemic thinking uses two categories of hypotheses:

1. *Re-telling:* A story or summary that expresses a meaning that is
    immediately comprehensible, understandable, and acceptable.

2. *The actual hypothesis:* An interpretation of parts of a meaning, which has more detail and nuances than the factual conditions, because several assumptions are combined, and new understandings can be introduced.

Subordinate to this, *two forms* can be described:

1. A *general hypothesis* concerning the client's problem.
2. A *working hypothesis.*

The general hypothesis

The general hypothesis is an image or a metaphor created on the basis of information and observations about the participants' behaviour, intentions, expressed thoughts, and internal relations.

The working hypothesis

The working hypothesis is the consultant's own tool, which may provide a *preliminary* model for summarizing and clarifying what is going on in the system. The purpose of forming the working hypothesis is to achieve a preliminary understanding of the nature and scope of the problem. The working hypothesis therefore contributes to maintaining the consultant's attention and curiosity. It aims to create a cognitive change and to contribute to making the consultant alter her perspective in a constant process. In some situations, the working hypothesis is only a part of the consultant's inner dialogue, in others the systemic consultant may use the hypothesis *explicitly* in an open forum. Therefore, hypotheses often include questions. The hypotheses are *not linear* (cause →️ effect) in structure, but circular. They provide the consultant with a "world map" of the interaction that reflects the locked-up situation.

The hypothesis draws on several sources for its contents. One source is the information that the consultant gains through her interactions with the client-system. Another source is the consultant's previous experiences with other assignments, and a third, the consultant's theoretical understanding. It is of no interest to which theoretical school the consultant belongs. Other theoretical approaches may provide important sources of inspiration for the consultant's hypotheses. The essential aspect is the consultant's ability to tie relevant theory, experience, and knowledge together and to do this in a developing and enthusiastic way.

An important element in the formation of hypotheses is to understand the implications of the way that the events appear, and to include many *varieties of possible understandings*. The purpose of forming hypotheses is to give the participants a sense of being understood. In this way, the formation of hypotheses focuses on the combination and the link between understanding and options.

Campbell, Draper, and Huffington (1991a) use hypotheses to be able to work with:

1.   conflicts between individual needs and the organization's current needs and life cycle

2.   relational conflicts that occur as a consequence of change or threats of change

Information gathering is used for forming hypotheses. A key perspective in the application of hypotheses is to shed light on a *"gain–loss discussion"*, where a typical question would be: "What might be the gains and losses to the individual or the organization in changing a given behaviour?" The process of hypothesizing draws on three *different dimensions* (Campbell, Coldicott, & Kinsella, 1994):

1.   clarity or ambiguity in definition of relationships

2.   time—past, present, and future

3.   discrepancies between beliefs and actions

The consultant who uses this method in forming systemic hypotheses has to assume an inquisitive and curious attitude to the situation or problem. An inquisitive attitude requires a distance to the situation where, on the mental plane, the consultant is able to detach herself from the current perception of the problem definition. Campbell, Coldicott, and Kinsella (1994) call this a "meta-position". In systemic practice, the meta-position is the position of being fully and completely involved and simultaneously uninvolved! It is in this frame of mind that the consultant forms her hypotheses. The process of hypothesizing also enables the consultant to maintain a comprehensive view and a reflected distance. By putting forth different hypotheses about a problem or situation, the consultant gives the client a new perspective on the difficulties. The client gets an opportunity to be an observer to his own situation and, in a psychological sense, gets a safe space for viewing things from outside/above/below. This gives the client an emotional space for distancing himself from the situation.

The consultant must *avoid considering or accepting hypotheses as true and complete explanations*. Hypotheses, rather, are the basis for forming concepts and meanings that can be shared with others and for shifting experiences from that which is grasped at a given moment to what is considered at the next moment. They do not work as conclusions to complex situations. Cecchin points out that the consultant's attitude towards hypotheses must be governed by her *ethical and moral working principles*, as she decides which hypotheses to present to the client (Cecchin & Stratton, 1991). He also points out that the consultant should not "fall in love with" particular hypotheses, but, on the contrary, should retain a playful, experimental, irreverent attitude to the hypotheses. When hypotheses cease to be useful, one should be "faithless" to them and create new ones. With *irreverence*, Cecchin means an unorthodox and creative stance, where one challenges one's own and other people's ideas and understandings in a constant process. This way, the consultant can avoid having the hypotheses appear as ready-made solutions, which reduces the consultant's risk of winding up in a position based on power and expertise in relation to the client-system (Cecchin & Stratton, 1991).

Hypotheses, therefore, are more than simple and correct decisions, which is why it is useful for the consultant to establish many hypotheses, even if they are mutually contradictory.

When the consultant formulates hypotheses, she should pay attention to how they might influence the client. This occurs typically in those cases where the consultant clings to a particular hypothesis and wants to lead the client down a certain path. If the client takes over the consultant's hypothesis uncritically, there is a risk that the hypothesis might not differ from the client's own thinking. This will not provide the difference in thinking that is the primary purpose of the systemic hypothesis (Huffington, 1996). The purpose of forming hypotheses is to create an *appreciable* difference from the belief system that the client both produces and is a part of. The art is to remain in touch with the client's experiences and continually compare the client's reactions with one's own ideas, while continuing to pay attention to one's own thinking. By co-ordinating, expanding, elaborating, and listening during the feedback phase, the consultant can take the formation of hypotheses to a *higher level of meaning*. This way, the client can acquire a new and different understanding of the problematic situations as well as a new set of options.

Hypothesizing is a *creative* activity that develops in a spiralling, progressive process. As mentioned earlier, the process of hypothesizing draws on unconscious mental images and intuitive processes, whose goal is to produce an integrated picture from the fragmented information, so that first the consultant and later the client may have an "aha" experience. What is important is not whether the client likes the hypotheses, but whether he will get involved in them and play along. If the hypothesis meets with resistance because it confronts the participant in a way that causes emotional aversion and dislike, the consultant has to *change* the hypothesis to "defuse" the aspects that provoke and rephrase the hypothesis to raise new questions.

Through the formation of hypotheses, those in the client-system have an opportunity to see how differently a situation is viewed and experienced when different persons are involved. This reflects the fact that experiences are interpreted by individuals and are therefore not accessible for straightforward, conventional approaches. Therefore, the formation of hypotheses alters the more oblique interactions and renders them visible.

Positive reframing is a method that originally came from systemic family therapy. The concept can be illustrated as follows. Two men look through the prison bars; one sees mud, the other stars. The point is that one man sees the problem, while the other man sees hope. The purpose of positive reframing is to give the problem a positive slant. The problem at hand is interpreted and understood in a constructive way, so that the participants free up resources for taking action. The positive reframing must be different from the client's own phrasing, but no so far removed from it that the client cannot use it to alter existing understandings and behaviour. If the hypotheses are too far removed, they will appear to be unrelated to the issue. If they are too similar to the system's own hypotheses, they provide no new information. As a first step, the consultant has to uncover the client's own explanation of his current situation. The client's own hypotheses will usually be linear (see section 5.2).

The consultant must focus her attention on looking for something else—that is, finding new *connections* that were not known previously. Circular questioning brings forth information that can form the basis for the consultant's hypotheses. The reframing aims at making the constructive aspects of the problem visible in order to "detoxify" the client from bad experiences and feelings of being locked in, of suffering and being a victim of the problem.

It is important to remember that there is no "right" way to form hypotheses. One has to build a repertoire, vary it, explore and seek new ways, accept inspiration, and play along. One has to be willing to take risks and challenge both one's own thinking and that of others. One has to elaborate on the questions and ideas that lead to the hypotheses. Systemic hypotheses build on a development process, which gets increasingly complex, as the insight into the various relations grows.

5.6   *Interventions*
                          [Kit Sanne Nielsen]

The commissioner expects the consultant's efforts to lead to changes in a given situation or problem. The commissioner wants the consultant to provide interventions on which the participants can act. In systemic thinking, the attitude to this is that, essentially, the client holds the key to the solution, while the consultant's role is to be a catalyst for the process.

The interventions that the consultant applies in her practical work usually range from simple psychological advice to interventions of greater dynamic complexity. Such interventions may include:

- *Qualitative interviews* with people, individually or in groups. Here, the consultant gathers data, forms hypotheses, and establishes a framework for the next steps in the process.

- *Passing on information* (that is otherwise not disseminated) *to key persons in the organization.*

- *Bringing people together* who normally do not meet and talk, and acting as a *mirror* or a *translator* in these meetings.

- *Clarifying roles, ground rules, demands, and expectations between people* with different (hierarchical) authority.

- *Guiding the formation of visions and goals,* so that the system acquires a shared context that becomes comprehensible to the members of the organization.

The consultant chooses which interventions to employ after she has heard, comprehended, and interpreted the messages. One or more hypotheses are then formulated and applied in order to examine whether they make sense to the client. The client-system can then use the hypotheses to discover new options by doing something different from what had been done previously. One might also say that in systemic thinking interventions and the formation of hypotheses are integrated processes. The very goal with the consultant's interventions is to promote the organization's own *autonomous ability for adaptation and learning* through this feedback process. Sometimes the client does not agree with the consultant's new version. In that case, the consultant should be humble and express that the client is the real expert, and that the consultant is only trying to look at things in another light. This often has a positive effect.

I have found the systemic approach applicable in contexts of this nature, because it promotes the organization's own skills and ability to make decisions. Both circular questioning and the consultant's neutrality have a strong effect on the client.

The consultant's choice of intervention is based on her intuitive impression of what will be appropriate and useful to the client. Interventions should therefore be adjusted to fit the organizational entity that is the *object of the intervention*: Is it top management exclusively—or is it a particular manager and, if so, who? Is it a management team, an entire department, a special group, and so forth? The complex intervention looks different from the linear intervention. An example of a linear problem statement is when the general view in the organization is that "the manager is incompetent and has to change" or "the staff is bickering and has to learn to speak up".

The systemic perspective supplements the linear approach by offering techniques for seeing things from a "how-perspective". The systemic perspective points to possible explanations and offers interpretations that can elucidate the *"pattern of repetition"* or the *"pattern of maintenance"*. At the same time as this is being made visible, a new frame of reference is being introduced.

The following section describes five basic methods for intervention. They are inspired by McCaughan and Palmer (1994) and by Cooperrider (1990):

1. positive reframing
2. directions for action
3. containment or maintenance of the status quo
4. reflections
5. metaphors

Positive reframing

In section 5.5, I described the concept of positive reframing in relation to the formation of hypotheses. The purpose of positive reframing as a general form of intervention is to shed light on the participants' own possibilities of utilizing their strong points and resources and of avoiding victimizing themselves in the face of other people's power and control. Interventions of this nature have a dual purpose. On the one hand, they aim to de-emphasize the negative and stressful aspects that keep the persons locked into a given situation (for example by assuming victims' roles). On the other hand, they are to offer a positive experience in contrast to the victimization. A positive reframing of a victim's role could be: being considerate and allowing others to have influence. Using positive reframing in interventions often mobilizes the person's vigour, responsibility, and obligation to take matters into his own hands and take action, because it provokes new reactions.

In his article, "Positive Image—Positive Actions", Cooperrider (1990) describes and discusses positive images and the impact and effect they have on people's organizational behaviour. The article's key issue is the way that positive mental phenomena, for example the placebo effect, can bring about resource-building positive predictions about the future developments of an organization. (The placebo effect is the medical phenomenon whereby a third to two-thirds of all patients will show marked physical and psychological improvement simply because they believe that they are given an effective treatment, even though they are only getting, for example, a sugar tablet. It is the patient's positive expectations about the treatment that produce the therapeutic effect.) The organizational agents' positive images, expectations, future dreams, or visualizations about the organization are powerful factors in improving the members' involvement and enthusiasm. If top management invites the staff members to take part in a dialogue about this, it may be the seed from which the affirmative ideas can grow.

Albert Einstein has stated that "Imagination is more important than knowledge" (Cooperrider, 1990). It is a fundamental human gift to be able to perceive our life in positive terms. Our quality of life increases when we are optimistic and positive about our personal development or the things we hope to accomplish. Cooperrider calls this "affirmative cognition" and describes it as a unique, self-initiating development process.

When we look to the horizon with our positive expectations, we can convince ourselves that positive events can occur for real. This allows us to mobilize our strength and actions in the direction of our wishes. This can promote social behaviour, the appreciation of other people's efforts (the Pygmalion experiment), confidence in one's own resources, and the belief that one is capable of putting in a better effort. The classical *Pygmalion* study demonstrated what happens when schoolteachers are told ahead of time that certain of their pupils are especially gifted, while certain others have a learning impediment. The schoolteachers developed a positive attitude towards the "good" pupils and a negative attitude towards the pupils whom they thought to be less gifted. In fact, all the pupils in the class were equally gifted and talented. As time went by, a marked difference occurred between the pupils. The pupils who met with a positive attitude developed further, while the pupils who were thought to be lagging actually did begin to fall behind. This phenomenon has been confirmed in many subsequent empirical studies (see Cooperrider, 1990).

Once I was a consultant to a department where we were working on improving the interactions within a group. I suggested that instead of looking at the cooperation problems, we should look at the members' positive experiences with each other. The questions that the group had to work with were as follows: What has worked well in our cooperation? What have we done to make it work? What are our hopes and dreams about the way that we want to cooperate? What high points have we shared? What creates a good atmosphere in our group? The consultant chooses this approach not in order to avoid talking about the negative aspects, but in order to use a different language and talk about the problems in a *constructive and energy-building* way. This ensures an affirmative and supportive language, which may inspire the participants, give them faith in their own possibilities, and bring out the resources that function in parallel with the problem areas in their day-to-day cooperation. When the group focuses on this and becomes aware which situations are life-giving, they become capable of improving the emotional climate in the group. This enables the members to boost their optimism, hope, caring, joy, and altruism. The next question is what the group should do once the cooperation works well, and how it can transfer these actions and ideas to the areas where it wants change.

Another example of the power of positive thinking comes from a consultation with a management team, where the managers wanted to discuss their roles and look at how they were perceived, personally, by the employees in the organization. At one point, the group was debating whether the top manager was too charismatic or, as he put it himself, "was outshining the other managers". At this point I intervened and suggested that he discuss with the other managers instead how they might "step out into the light" with him and share in the desired image. This gave him the opportunity to be an appreciative and rewarding manager, who was willing to "share his charisma" with the other managers. In this way, the other managers, too, would have "affirmative soil" for appreciating themselves, which could result in a more positive attitude, both about their own potential and about the potential of their staff members.

Directions for action

The purpose of this form of intervention is to *guide the client*. The consultant provides rather detailed and specific directions for how the client may act differently or show a different attitude in a specific situation. The Milan method called this *"directions for rituals"* (Tomm, 1989).

It may appear contradictory to prescribe specific actions within the framework of the systemic method. The explanation is that the directions are to be seen as a proposal for intervention that may shed light on an inappropriate pattern in the relationships between two or more persons. This may help the client to discover the problematic aspects of the situation. This new insight creates clarity about, for example, games and distributions of roles and tasks, which may have become frozen. At the same time, they also realize that these patterns have developed—and continue to develop—as the result of interactive processes in which they themselves are involved. The ritual is a proposed experiment—not necessarily because it needs to be carried out, but because it adds a new perspective to a given interaction between people. One example is a staff group that is unable to solve a practical problem: Who is supposed to get the paper for the photocopier, clean up the common kitchen area, and so forth? The manager is irritated that the staff cannot just be adults about it and work it out. The controversy has existed for a long time, and the manager has told the staff that they have to find a reasonable solution. In this situation, the consultant can intervene by suggesting that the manager and the group together work out a roster, which describes in detail who does what, how often, and how. The suggestion can make the manager and the group aware that they have to help each other work things out in behavioural terms, and that sometimes the manager has to act with authority, providing clear directions and guidelines for his staff. At the same time, the staff members are made aware that through their own lack of responsibility they are appealing to a stronger management style.

An important aspect of rituals is that they allow the consultant to make key role expectations explicit by describing specific behaviour patterns. If the group and the manager do not acknowledge the ritual and the behaviour does not change, the issue of role ambiguity can be made more evident in the continued consultation. In this respect, the ritual can be a means for confronting the participants with inherent and unacknowledged patterns and games.

Containment

This intervention technique is used with the purpose of *temporarily keeping the person from making decisions and acting*. By encouraging questions, analysis, and hypotheses, he is allowed to focus more deeply on the problem and is also invited to become *his own consultant*. The purpose is to promote learning, analysis, and an understanding of the connections involved. It also gives him an opportunity to face the problem and cope with the emotional pressure that would normally make him act. Members of the organization learn to *handle* the potentially ambiguous *emotions, anxieties, irritation*, and so forth that the problem causes. I have discovered a similar method by watching the way that a group analyst intervenes. Here, the therapist holds back, listens, and empathizes, giving the participants an opportunity to articulate their concerns, which seems to have a therapeutic effect in itself. This position often improves the communication within the group and promotes a sense of community (Rice & Scott Rutan, 1987). One example is a management team that wants to get rid of a difficult employee. Several of the managers find it hard to cooperate with this person, and they are annoyed with his behaviour. The consultant is able to assume a stance of understanding and acceptance, which gives the managers the space to handle the emotional tension. This has a soothing effect. Additionally, the consultant advises the management team not to make any decisions to dismiss the employee before there has been a rational inquiry into whether or not the difficult employee should be let go.

Reflections

As we have discussed before (chapter 1), problem-owners are often very concerned about the problematic situation and focus all their energy on it. The challenge before the consultant is to focus instead on the client-system's hopes and wishes for change. Both the consultant's hypotheses and the participants' reflections are forms of intervention that can bring about change. The challenge is to focus one's own thoughts on how conditions might improve, "if only . . ." , as this is a far better vehicle for progress.

The consultant's task is to free the system from the context-dependent experiences and to initiate a progressive transition towards other points of view. When the consultant works alone and without a reflecting team, she can change position, instead, by contemplating the events from the different positions of the members. By reflecting on the basis of these different positions, several versions of questions and experiences are made visible, and the participants can later have a dialogue about these. The consultant's reflections spring from the most important of the ideas, impressions, and themes that the participants have verbalized. The reflections are a commentary on what the consultant has heard and provide her feedback on this to the participants. It is often useful and very effective to discuss the emotions that the participants have in relation to the perceived problems. These emotions are often not expressed, and when the consultant expresses the potential emotions in connection with the problem, the participants are able to relate to their own feelings more openly. In her reflections, the consultant can ask questions or make remarks that are surprising or unusual. This may enable the participants to wonder too, and this may make them ask new and different questions about the problem.

In chapter 3, I described how I had used a model for the reflecting team. In order to attain a more detailed picture of how the staff members perceived the cooperation problems, I interviewed one person from the group, while the others listened. The rest of the group was divided into three reflecting teams. The purpose of this was to create listening positions, reflecting positions, and dialogue positions. The individual team member listened during the interview, so that there was room for other information for the person to listen to. This information was revealed once the reflecting team began their reflecting dialogue about what they had heard. The consultant needs to provide very specific instruction concerning the exchange of reflections.

I have made it a habit to use the following guidelines for instructing the team members:

1. Speak in constructive and positive terms and avoid criticism or derision.

2. Let the thoughts flow freely and make room for wondering.

3. Begin sentences with expressions like, for example: "I wonder what . . .", "I wonder why . . .", "What might happen if . . .".

4. Expand on the ideas of other team members. The point is not to reach an agreement, but to construct different thoughts, approaches, and questions.

5. The more versions, the better.

6. A first step could be: How do we perceive what the interviewee is saying? What effect does it have on us and on others inside and outside the system?

7. Try to provide guidance: What might it be a good idea for the interviewee to do—for example: If I were X, I would. . . . What are other people's experiences with a given solution? What ideas does the team have? What sort of support would be available?

The team's reflecting discussion provides input for the next interview. The interviewee is under the same rules as the reflecting team: while the reflecting team is debating, the interviewee listens and is allowed to make notes. Usually, the interviewee is fascinated with the constructive and productive discussion that unfolds. It is important that the consultant maintain to the interviewee that comments and reflections that he makes afterwards should be the points that he found "provokingly interesting". The interviewee is not obliged to comment on everything. The interviewee is also not allowed to interrupt the interaction in the reflecting team, so he has no opportunity of convincing others of his point of view. From this observing position the interviewee develops a deeper understanding of his dilemma or relationship with the system and is able to detach himself from the problem as well as contemplating the problem from the outside (see Campbell et al., 1991a). See also Karl Tomm (1987b), who offers a very detailed treatment of the reflecting questioning technique.

Metaphors

This is an intervention technique that I have found very effective to use. If the participants wish to understand their organization, this should be approached with the understanding that it is useful to view the organization as a *complex, ambiguous, and paradoxical entity* (see Morgan, 1986).

Metaphors can be effective ways of *handling complexity*. In this context, metaphors function as revealing and probing images of paradoxical situations. At the same time, the metaphors function as a communication vehicle for what has been perceived but not yet put into words. It will often be useful to employ the organization's own language and metaphors—for example: "leave all hope behind" or "this is a madhouse". The consultant may then elaborate on the metaphor. Or new metaphors can be introduced in order to present an image from which the participants can develop new associations (as I do in my case about Peter's role in the group, in chapter 3).

The purpose of metaphors is to be a means for explaining experiences or behaviour if it is difficult for the participants to express emotions and experiences directly (grief, anger, loss). Metaphors constitute a *pictorial language* for expressing an interpretation of certain conditions. This helps the participants to re-interpret and cope with their problems. Metaphors may provide a common ground for a shared understanding and for the creation of a network that an otherwise divided group may use as a platform for action.

There is a close link between the way people think and the way they act. Therefore, many organizational problems stem from the members' way of thinking. When the consultant varies and qualifies her interventions, new ways of thinking are introduced. Members of the organization are given a possibility to alter their understanding and to find new ways to act and, thus, an opportunity to make the changes that they wish for.

CHAPTER SIX

The consultant's cognitive processes in practice: when two consultants work together

Kit Sanne Nielsen

How I learned to be an organizational consultant

Consultants are practitioners, and we carry out our activities through direct and indirect communication. The activities take place through many types of actions, in which we present our theories, methods, and reflections to others. Language, meaning, and action are the key areas about which we ourselves also continue to learn.

The issue I want to address here is how I, as a psychologist and a consultant, developed this competence.

When looking back at the years that I have practised as an organizational consultant, I have been in frequent contact with other consultants—consultants who, like me, work as external consultants or as internal consultants (human resources consultants or educational consultants). As a person, I am extrovert, seek contact with others, am action-oriented, and want to test my ideas and learn new things. I prefer challenges, change, inspiration, and creative tasks. My work needs to be meaningful and to present opportunities for self-development. I have always had a strong interest in and identification with my profession.

I embarked on a traditional career as a psychologist working as a government employee in a hospital system. This is where I got my practical experience and additional clinical training. During the first years, I worked with diagnostics, psychological investigation methods, group therapy, individual therapy, couple counselling, and with supervision and advice for the nursing staff. Today I recognize that the background in adult therapy and self-therapy that I also acquired during these years has been an important part of the foundation for my work as a consultant.

The learning and training that I went through as a clinical psychologist was rooted in psychodynamic thinking about subconscious processes. As a therapist I focused on understanding the dynamic processes in the individual case history in order to understand how these became manifest as deep mental patterns and emotional memories. At the time, my main focus was on learning how I might intervene as a therapist to change the code of the past and the client's expectations and self-image.

Later, I worked with individuals and couples in a private practice, and I provided supervision to professionals involved with treatment: psychologists, therapists, social workers, and so forth. My work changed from a direct client–therapist relationship into a role as consultant. This new role provided an opportunity to observe the therapeutic relationship and to reflect on the relationships between therapist and client, which pushed me in new theoretical and methodological directions. It was in connection with this that I became acquainted with systemic theory and practice. Working with the supervision of treatment professionals had brought me into the treatment organization, which in turn inspired me to work with the treatment system. I learned that the observations and tools that I used for supervision could be transferred to organizations, but that I had to supplement my psychological knowledge and experience with an understanding of organizational theory. I was inspired by the learning I had gained from the Tavistock Institute, with regard both to group analysis and to the systemic method. The Tavistock Institute was founded in 1946; it carried out research and teaching about change and

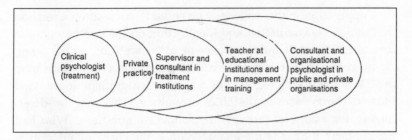

FIGURE **6.1.**   **My path to organizational consultation**

development in groups and organizations with group analysis as its frame of reference.

It was through working with these thoughts, ideas, and methods that I developed my practice as a consultant.

In the years that followed, I participated in workshops, received supervision myself, and cooperated with other organizational consultants in an exchange of experience and literature. I participated in training sessions, in Denmark and abroad, in order to expand my knowledge and competence in the area of organizational psychology. During this learning process, I worked as a practitioner involved in teaching, management training, and consultancy to large and small public and private companies. It was during this process that I met other consultants, who were later to be my colleagues and working partners. It has always been of great importance to me, as a solo consultant, to establish a network that lets me find partners for assignments as well as ideas, inspiration, advice, and guidance for my own work. (See Figure 6.1.)

Cooperating with other consultants:
Similarities and discrepancies

In my experience, consultation can be a lonely occupation, unless one finds other consultants with whom to cooperate. There is a danger of seizing up, professionally, and of using up one's own internal resources—burning out. One has to be able to exchange ideas with others. It is through feedback and dialogue with professional partners that one has a chance to internalize new learning.

Cooperation with a colleague on equal terms is often a relation that builds on fascination and idealization on the one hand and a fear of losing one's independence or of competition on the other: "If he is better than me, then my clients might choose him over me." When working together on a specific assignment, it is a good idea to clarify who is the chief consultant. This may be determined, for example, through the following questions: Who had the contact? Whose is the client? Who is the client's contact person? There needs to be an agreement for every assignment as well as unambiguous rules.

Define the relationship with the commissioner from the outset. Who is in charge of the process? This person has to keep the other consultant informed and handle the overall contact with the commissioner. Who writes the invoice to the client? How is the fee to be divided? It is important to sort out the economic aspects from the beginning, to avoid later controversies over this issue.

The partnerships that I describe here are based on experiences that I have made over time. I find that the interaction with other consultants promotes the client's own development and learning. This is not to say that the cooperation is without its problems. I address the problem areas in more detail in the section below.

Working with a partner holds both benefits and drawbacks, as shown in Table 6.1.

Working with a colleague can improve the consultant's self-understanding and, in the long term, can help the consultant to develop an empathy with the client's reactions, feelings, and attitudes. This learning process gives the consultant an opportunity to project herself onto others and identify with them without trying to change them. In stressful situations, the consultant has to be able to react in a calming and non-judgemental manner, as this also has a calming effect on the participants.

Cooperating with colleagues who have a different professional background: discrepancy

The consultants with whom I have cooperated fall into two main categories: psychologists and other related professional groups.

Table 6.1. Working with a partner

Benefits	Drawbacks
Having different positions means having different views and actions. This gives the client-system more nuances and options.	If the consultants begin to compete with each other, for example in relation to the commissioner, the quality of the work may suffer.
One can learn from one another—expand one's methods and knowledge.	Cases where one feels that there is no learning or inspiration.
The client-system has the benefit of two resource persons.	The relationship between the two consultants takes up too much room and drains energy from the client-system.
It is possible to share the workload, which reduces the risk of burnout.	Dual effort—both are doing the same work, but in different ways.
There is feedback on one's role, interventions and style.	Feedback is perceived as criticism, causing a defensive response.

The latter is comprised mostly of people with a background in the *humanities*, in *law*, or in *business administration*.

The professional *discrepancy* has meant that we have had different qualifications; it has been a benefit that, as a *consultancy team*, we have covered a larger area of knowledge. This cooperation has been useful in external and internal management training and organizational development programmes, where we have acted as consultants, teachers, and trainers.

I have represented the area of organizational psychology and the interactive aspect with a focus on the processes of human change and rejuvenating forms of cooperation in the organization. My colleague will have had her competence in the area of corporate strategy, where organizational goals, structural change, and job-specific issues have been in focus.

It was a learning experience for me, because I gained knowledge from an area outside my own educational qualifications. In relation to the specific assignment at hand, it also meant that I knew that the resources that the client might need would be present. The new knowledge improved my ability to place my psychological knowledge within an organizational context. It made me realize exactly where to draw the defining boundaries for my learning and where I wanted my strong points to be. It also taught me to focus on the areas that interest me, without any hopes or ambitions of mastering the entire spectrum.

When two psychologists cooperate: Similarities and feedback

In other contexts, the cooperation with other psychologists has been useful—for example, in connection with activities concerning personal development, cooperation training, and conflict solving. These activities have taken place in management training sessions, departmental seminars, or consultations. In this connection, I will confine myself to cooperation in consultations.

When the cooperation takes place between two colleagues within the same field, a *professional similarity* comes into existence—a shared dialogue about the psychological understandings in the consultation. The teamwork may function as a *professional feedback loop*, where we are challenged on the issue of our relationship with the customer. The reflections that we have established together have given us a deeper understanding of our roles and our own behaviour as consultants. Because we share the same frame of reference, the feedback becomes more personal and challenges our self-images. We act "irreverently" towards each other (Cecchin, Lane, & Ray, 1992) by challenging our own ideas and logic. In order to do this, one has to be able to receive the feedback and be willing to examine one's own ideas and motivation. If accepted, this sort of irreverent feedback can improve one's own flexibility and willingness to take risks and to express emotions, controversies, and fantasies. It will also improve one's ability to examine one's own motives, thinking, and reasoning. This is a rather confrontational relationship, where someone else questions one's strategies. In my experience, one has to learn to utilize this and see it as an extremely valuable chance for developing one's own role as a consultant instead of fearing violations of one's personal space. On the one hand, one might perceive the comments as criticism, rejection, and uncalled-for interference. On the other, it is beneficial to have this check-up from a colleague, if one wants to improve as a process consultant. When acting as a consultant who needs to understand and intervene in organizational dilemmas, it is a great learning experience to be monitored by another person. And in my experience, a fellow psychologist (or a colleague who is a trained therapist) has the ability to ask the most probing and relevant questions. Obviously, one has to trust the intentions and qualifications of one's colleague in a relationship of mutual trust. A partnership of this nature increases the depth, whereas a cooperation with a colleague from an adjacent area increases the width.

Cooperating with internal consultants

Differences between the external and the internal consultant

Compared with the partnership with another external consultant, cooperating with an internal consultant creates a completely different situation. The external consultant and the internal consultant have different backgrounds for their work.

The internal consultant is involved in the organizational hierarchy and policies. The internal consultant has to adhere to and support the corporate goals, and there are certain tasks that he *must* take on. The staff of a human resources department will have to act in a particular way towards the managers and employees of the organization. They have to follow certain procedures and chains of command. One has to communicate in a certain way, depending on the positions and styles of the various managers, and so forth. The activities or programmes that one is expected to carry out and develop have to be carried out in a close dialogue with the affected persons (management or staff). Often these activities are decided by others, and this can place the internal consultant on the horns of a dilemma: he has an assignment that is sponsored by others (for example, top management), and he has to motivate, cajole, or force the participants to accept it. On the one hand, the internal consultant has to submit to the hierarchy during negotiations; on the other hand, he has to obtain the acceptance and consent of the participants, who will often disagree.

The external consultant is confronted with these issues too, but not to the same degree. She has a much larger market, and her job holds more freedom. If necessary, she can choose to turn down an assignment, an option that the internal consultant does not have to nearly the same extent.

The external consultant is free to ask questions and commands a wide knowledge base from many different organizations, whereas the internal consultant has her local knowledge and a basic knowledge as a participant and member of the organization. The internal consultant will be able to spot the need for consultation at an early time and thus become the catalyst for a desire for change. This makes the internal consultant a stakeholder in the organizational change, which can ease the implementation phase, because the internal consultant will be able to utilize her knowledge of the organization and the power structures and policies to implement the changes.

Block (1981) offers an overview of the differences between the internal and the external consultant. I have made some additions to his model, as shown in Table 6.2.

In processes of organizational change, the internal consultant has often observed a series of conflicts, but for a number of reasons is reluctant about being the consultant on the process herself. She may feel that she lacks the objectivity or neutrality, perhaps because she has allied herself earlier with a certain group of people (for example the employees or management). It is exactly because of this different position that the external consultant may be called for.

Who does what?

As an external consultant, one has to define a relationship with the internal consultant based on a clear distribution of roles. At the same time, one should not be blind to the fact that the internal consultant is a part of the client-system. This may often be the first

Table 6.2. Comparison between the internal and the external consultant

	Internal consultant	External consultant
Favourite expressions	Measurement	That raises an interesting issue
	Long run	Fundamental and underlying
	Quick	Deal
	Practical	Working through
	Objectives	Dilemma
	Background	Model
	Cost	Implications
		Reassess at some point in the process
Personal life	Reasonably stable, responsible and rewarding	A chaotic and unpredictable life
Fantasy life	Envious of the external consultant's freedom and variation	Envious of the internal consultant's continuity and stability
Underlying fears	Being ignored, rejected and treated as unimportant	Being ignored, rejected and treated as unimportant
Dilemma	Perceives herself as being outside the client-system	Thinks that the internal consultant is a part of the client-system
Dream position	To be a co-consultant on the project and be briefed by the external consultant	To be free to move around in the system and maintain her right to withhold information

and, perhaps, the biggest challenge in cooperating with an internal consultant. I find that, usually, the internal consultant attempts to establish a close, confidential professional relationship with me in my role as the external consultant. This invitation for a close professional relationship is tempting but nevertheless problematic. The problematic aspect is that the internal consultant may obtain information from me, as the external consultant, which he may use inappropriately. My observations and hypotheses could potentially be taken back to the organization and used against the participants with whom I work. It is important to be allowed to keep one's observations to oneself while working on the problems, as, otherwise, they may be taken for expert truths. In that case, the external consultant runs the risk of becoming entangled in the organizational politics, and before she knows it, she is "stuck". This means that the consultant loses her ability to assume the neutral and reflecting position that is a prerequisite for the consultation.

Another important issue is how to involve the internal consultant in the process—that is, to what extent and in what capacity he is to participate in the actual consultation. I have never experienced the internal consultant to actually broach this issue himself. But as an external consultant, one needs to define the roles precisely. Unless the external consultant is already a familiar face in the organization, the internal consultant will often participate in a number of activities, meetings, planning, and so forth. When drawing up the contract about the consultation, it therefore has to be defined to what extent the internal consultant is to be included, and what his role is going to be. This ensures that the internal and the external consultant as well as the department know the roles and the premises for them. It may be useful for the external consultant to have a position different from that of the internal consultant. But there may also be activities and situations, where the department or the client-system prefers to work with the external consultant alone, because they want an unbiased and neutral process management. This can also be addressed in the consultation, but perhaps that is not what should be the focus of attention.

Cooperation with the internal consultant is of the greatest importance in the preliminary and initial stages of a consultation.

The internal consultant possesses inside knowledge about the organization, which may be utilized in tailoring a management training programme, so that the programme can meet the participants' learning needs, backgrounds, and interests. Still, however, the external consultant has to meet the participants in person to interview them about their wishes and expectations. This is necessary to make sure that the training activities can be challenging and match the participants' needs, so that the external consultant can establish a direct psychological contract with the participants.

As an external consultant, one needs for the internal consultant to:

1. describe what she perceives to be the problems that others have;
2. provide her own description of what she perceives the problem to be, and what she has done in relation to the problem so far;
3. relate what others (management, for example) expect of the problem solving process;
4. provide information about the expectations concerning time and scope of activities (resources, economy).

A cooperation between an external and an internal consultant requires a very clear distribution of roles. In the case described in chapter 3, the functions of the internal consultant were as follows: the internal consultant established the contact with the department, represented by the manager. He summarized briefly what the organization had done to address the problem so far. This briefing included the history and some thoughts and ideas as to what the problem might be as well as his opinion as to what the organization might need from a solution. This enabled me to understand the expectations of top management and to compare these with the expectations expressed by the department and the manager. Any discrepancies or similarities between these versions could form the basis for the first of my working hypotheses.

In the case in chapter 3, the internal consultant was the consultant's contact person, and John (the manager) and his staff were the participants. John's department was the sponsor. The internal consultant had handled the initial talks with the manager and the individual members of staff, and John's boss had approved the use of an external consultant for solving the problem.

The internal consultant did not want to handle the situation himself, because he did not feel that he had an adequate picture of the problem. Besides, he felt that there was a need for a consultant who could go into *depth* with the internal relationships among the participants. He was not sure that he could manage this task. I was selected, because I had a psychological background, knew the organization well, and had previously handled tasks of this nature.

In this specific case, the agreement covered the following aspects:

1. how I was to be introduced to John and his staff;
2. with whom the contract should be made, and how we were to clarify the expectations and initiate the process;
3. how I was to gather information and data in order to understand the problems and form working hypotheses;
4. constraints concerning activities, time, working methods, and seminars, including the cost of the entire consultation—alternatively, if occasional consultation was found to be more appropriate, it would be defined as how many there would be and at what hourly rate; it also set an approximate deadline for when these constraints were to be defined;
5. a list of the methods that might be used in the process—for example, a systemic approach in combination with process consultation, climate survey, Myers–Briggs Type Indicator (Myers & Myers, 1993), methods for monitoring goals, and so forth.

The role of the internal consultant was to be a part of the client-system, but with respect for the special staff function that he held. This meant that he could receive all the information he needed by maintaining a dialogue with the department's manager. In the course of the process, he would also be able to share his thoughts about the situation with me, and I could then provide sparring on his views. I could make a situation report by briefly stating how far we were into the process (for example: currently I am interviewing the staff—without revealing the content of the interviews). In other words, I was in charge of the process, and only when the participants and I had agreed that my involvement had ended could he take over.

As the external consultant, I was responsible for ensuring the freedom and the space to work with the department without interference from the internal consultant. It was also my responsibility to get the support from the human resources department for addressing the problems. The internal consultant's dilemma was whether he trusted me to be able to work within the framework of the company's human resources policy.

The consultant's own learning: the qualitative leap

In order to learn, one has to accept, on an existential level, that there is something valuable outside oneself that one needs. This means that one has to acknowledge the existence of something valuable in the outside world. The opposite of this is envy or frustration stemming from not already representing every desirable value. In other words, one has to overcome the obstacle of confronting one's own lack of knowledge. One has to recognize that it is possible to learn from others and tone down one's sense of self-sufficiency.

The consultant should strive not to fall in love with her own ideas or get married to her hypotheses. As Cecchin, Lane, and Ray (1991) put it, one should only flirt with them. By putting oneself in a different position in professional cooperation, one learns to remain constantly curious and inquisitive towards one's work. David Campbell states that the consultant runs a risk by placing herself outside the comfort zone in every new situation. He recommends that the consultant move from a position of security and comfort to a position of inquisitive confusion. In her own process of learning and inquiry, the systemic consultant keeps up an ongoing debate with herself and others. It is hard work to remain constantly flexible and break up habitual thinking in order to assume a so-called *constructively opportunist position*, where one asks questions, examines differences, and reflects on the reactions and self-images of the participants (Campbell, Coldicott, & Kinsella, 1994). In my opinion exactly the same method can be used internally by the consultant team to reveal or disclose the consultants' own habitual thinking.

This presents several dilemmas, as a given practice and working style is usually based on a very independent style. It is typical for consultants to feel a little superior and self-sufficient. There is a downside to this self-sufficiency. Consultants strive to achieve perfection in their work, and they are easily hurt if they do not receive proper recognition. Facing a situation that one cannot immediately take in can cause insecurity. Typically, one may try to cover it up (lest the clients notice any flaws or shortcomings). Instead, it is far easier to talk about clients or colleagues having problems or going into a state of resistance. The strong performance drive that consultants have may prevent them from *introspection* and from acknowledging their own weaknesses and learning points. The consultant's wish for success—quick and visible—thus forms an obstacle for her own learning.

Chris Argyris (1991) describes the roots of the *learning dilemma* in detail.

Academics and consultants are good at learning direct theory and methodology on their own. They process quickly and reproduce quickly. They are high achievers. Therefore, they have not learned from failure. This allows the consultant to avoid discussing or reflecting on her own actions, and she does not learn how to adapt her behaviour for similar future incidents. It may be the very way that the problem is defined and solved that is the source of the problem. Admitting one's own part in a mistake is a prerequisite to personal learning. By *intellectualizing* or *making excuses for* one's mistakes, one neglects to learn.

Consultants often compare themselves with others and are constantly trying to improve their own performance, but they do not like to acknowledge or discuss this. This *defensive reaction* is especially activated when the consultants receive critical or negative feedback on their own performance. They feel threatened. The fact that their performance was not as good as they had hoped or thought makes them feel guilty and inferior—especially when they are getting good money for their efforts! So, every time their direct learning strategies fail them, they assume a defensive stance, reject criticism, and throw the blame on someone else. Briefly put: their ability to learn disappears at the time when they need it the most (Argyris, 1991).

These reactions can be seen as a *defensive response* with the purpose of *self-protection*. The consultant tries to blame others for the mistakes that occurred. This manoeuvre lets the consultant direct the attention away from herself and from the aspects for which she is in some way responsible.

At management seminars I have emphasized countless times that managers have to be able to acknowledge mistakes and learn from them. Nevertheless, I have to admit that it is a difficult task for consultants, including myself, to live up to this demand. My conclusion is that the consultant needs to own up to her own *feeling of self-sufficiency* and work on it.

The consultant can receive supervision as part of her own learning process (see chapter 7) and, together with other consultants, she can learn how to change her own way of reasoning, thinking, and feeling. This requires facing the facts, confronting one's wishes, conscious as well as subconscious, and seeing the influence that one has on others. Through a more confrontational dialogue and sparring with a colleague, one can learn much about one's interaction with others. The consultant has to be willing to examine her own role and to see her own part and contributions in interactions. She has to question her own assumptions, observations, and selections, acknowledge her own subjective vantage point, and analyse the influence that this has on the client-system. It is through this sort of learning dialogue that the consultant gets the opportunity to *transform her own role as a consultant*. I will call this the *"quantum leap of learning"*.

The consultant's own process of searching and learning may also make her ask herself simple questions. She can then question her own feelings, what she thinks she should avoid doing, and what might happen if she did it anyway. This way, the consultant can maintain her position as a participating observer and help expand the client's understanding of the problem. The position that the consultant should assume should be "one down" instead of "one up" (see chapter 1). This is different from the expert's position, as he might appear to be "lecturing" the client. When assuming a "one down" position, one has to love asking naive questions, as these are the questions that challenge the system. This is to the client's benefit, because the positive and appropriate aspects of the situation can be considered along with other possible positions that might be equally appropriate.

In connection with certain assignments, I have found it very valuable, even necessary, to work together with a fellow consultant in relation to a group. That has made it possible to perceive the subconscious and underlying messages, emotions, and reactions that may occur during the process. The dialogue and processing that take place cannot be replaced with a study of books. In a team, it is possible to take a critical look at one's own reactions and learn how to intervene more effectively, as well as hypothesizing together about the problems in the group.

When two consultants work together, it is also, in my experience, easier to see through the defence mechanisms of the client-system. When working with conflicts and resistance to change, for example, one is exposed to *splitting*. Splitting is a psychological defence mechanism in which the participants project their own good and bad perceptions about the relationship onto others—for example, the consultants. The good projections may be represented through an *idealization*, in the hope that the consultant can *rescue the participants*, heal them, and bring them harmony and bliss. A bad projection occurs, for example, when the participants believe that the consultant is angry with them or in other ways plans to bring them discomfort. A group may project the good and the bad perceptions, respectively, onto one or both of the consultants. By switching roles and reflecting on the process, the consultation team can address the defence mechanisms and in various ways attempt to respond to (subconscious) appeals for help. The consultation team can address the group's contradictory wishes, and from their different perspectives and experiences the consultants can reflect on the meaning that the use of *splitting* has for the group or the organization. This minimizes the consultants' own stress level and defensiveness.

In consultations about development and change, one deals with participants who harbour feelings of both anger and anxiety. The participants will often attempt to escape these feelings by severing them from themselves and projecting them onto the consultant, the manager, or others in the organization. Through the consultant's empathy, understanding, calm, and reflection, the participants can reclaim their anger and anxiety, analyse these, and change their perception. Learning of this nature is extremely important when working with, for example, *resistance to change*, and as a consultant one should expect to be the target of negative emotions. If the consultant reacts with a lack of understanding and becomes indignant or angry, thus displaying her personal shortcomings, this will strengthen the participants' negative feelings instead of calming them. If this happens, the participants will not learn to understand their own reactions or defence mechanisms effectively, which again will keep the conflict alive. As a consultant, one is often surprised by the intensity of the participants' anger and even by one's own anger with the participants over their reaction. One might even get the feeling that one has been attributed a role in someone else's imaginary drama (Rice & Scott, 1987).

CHAPTER SEVEN

The consultant's cognitive processes in practice: receiving supervision

Gitte Haslebo

How I learned to be an organizational consultant

My path to working as a systemically inspired consultant to public and private companies has passed through numerous stages. There is a thread running through these stages, touching on my areas of interest and learning processes, which is only really discernible now, in retrospect.

Figure 7.1 is an illustration of the most important stages; the transitions to new stages are marked through changes concerning role, theory, method, and client-system.

Already in my student days, I was fascinated with organizational consultation. Near the end of my studies, I had the opportunity of studying in the United States for a year, and here I became acquainted with a wide array of writers within the human relations school. When I returned to Denmark, it was with an increased awareness of new trends in other countries. I read, with great enthusiasm, the books by, for example, Watzlawick, Beavin, and Jackson (1967), and was influenced by general communication theory and general systems theory. As a trainee at the Danish

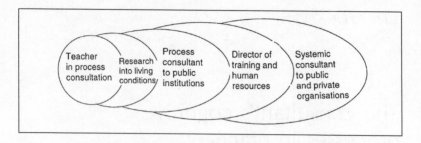

FIGURE 7.1.   My path to organizational consultation

Institute of Technology, which even then was the stronghold for the development and application of laboratory training (Høyrup, 1975), I developed a great interest in theoretical and methodological issues concerning how learning is created in situations with varying degrees of structure (Haslebo, 1973). After my traineeship, I was able to participate as junior consultant in a number of management courses and courses in personal development. It was in this setting that I had my first experiences as a process consultant.

When I was nearing my final exam as a psychologist, I was encouraged to apply for a teaching position in industrial and organizational psychology at the Psychology Laboratory, the University of Copenhagen. I took over the position before the spring semester in 1970 and enthusiastically began teaching organizational psychology and process consultation. Today I would say: a risky venture. But all went well. I experimented with experiential teaching methods, where the students were organized in groups that had to carry out "real" consultation assignments during the semester—they were "real" in the sense that each group had to try to do something useful for a client-system that the group itself was to contact and establish a formal as well as a psychological contract with; not quite so "real" in the sense that the consultation was mostly to be defined as a learning process for the students and was therefore free of charge to the client-system. From semester to semester, the classes grew. After five very satisfactory and educational semesters—and a total of nine years at the university as student and teacher, respectively—I felt that it was time for me to try my hand at something else.

During the next stage, I did research into living conditions (at the University Centre of Southern Jutland and in the Low Income Commission in Copenhagen)—eleven years in all. These years provided many useful experiences, on which I draw today in my work as a consultant: knowledge of quantitative and qualitative research methods, insight into everyday problems in an inter-disciplinary context, and an exploration of the interface between psychology and the adjacent areas of sociology, anthropology, history, and philosophy. My interest in the transition between "small" problems, as perceived by a specific population group, and the larger context was fostered—as was my interest in using data as feedback for the persons who had helped provide the data. It was also during this period that I began to see the writing pro-cess as a challenge, seeking to present complex issues in a simple, easily comprehensible, and captivating way. I became aware that writing and communicating a subject to my readers was a good way for me to learn.

After this I returned to the world of consultancy. In 1983 I obtained a position as a consultant in the Management Training Programme at the Danish School of Public Administration, where the first extensive management training programme (Course in Public Management) had just begun. The focus was on personal development in the manager role and the execution of many dif-ferent management tasks in the public sector, which was under-going major changes at the time. With two classes a year and 32 participants in each, the interest in the public sector spread more rapidly than we had expected. We were asked to handle projects in management development in those parts of the public sector from which the first participants had come. There was a great need in this area to develop a common understanding for the organization's situation and future and for handling the manage-rial role more professionally. I enthusiastically delved into these tasks, where I functioned as an external consultant. The issue that interested me the most was the possibilities for creating personal development processes in various organizational contexts and as an element in changing the organization. The types of consultations that I handled had to do with organizational development in connection with reorganization, team building in management teams, management training, and consultations with a view to developing policies and strategies.

Then followed five years when I worked, in turn, as manager of training and development and director of human resources. These years provided useful experience with human resources management, processes of change seen from inside the organization, sales and marketing, budgeting, and so forth. By "useful", I mean that not only have I had the experience of handling different management tasks, I have also personally experienced many of the challenges and dilemmas about which my clients tell me today.

In 1991, I felt that I was ready to establish my own business as an independent organizational consultant. I have been an independent consultant since then, interrupted only by a return to university, where again I taught organizational psychology. It was in connection with my change to being an independent consultant that I began to take more direct additional training within systemic thinking. A new world opened up to me, and new connections in life between old and new areas of interest became apparent. This new world consisted not only of new thoughts, but also of new clients and a new network of enthusiastic and highly qualified colleagues. Systemic thinking has provided additional and different perspectives on the various types of consultation with which I have worked and better opportunities for creating links between theory and practice, which I cherish. As part of this process, the idea arose of writing this book.

It is an important challenge in the work of the organizational consultant to plan consultation assignments in such a way that one has the necessary time and financial means for continually enhancing one's professional skills. This can be accomplished in a number of ways. I have benefited a great deal from participating in additional training and in groups for the exchange of experience with other consultants. Carrying out assignments together with other consultants has also been a source of experience (see chapter 6). I have explored the key questions—What works well? . . . and: What works less well?—through various ways of receiving systematic feedback from my client-systems. Last, but not least, I will mention the use of *supervision*, which can be an excellent way of gaining an insight into one's own cognition processes as a consultant.

I have had very good experiences with receiving continuous supervision as well as with receiving supervision at particularly difficult moments during specific consultations. Supervision has helped me assume a meta-position in relation to the consultation and the client-system and has provided a safe space for examining alternative links between practice and theory.

Supervision

Some assignments require the involvement of two consultants, but many are solo assignments. Being alone on an assignment means both handling all the contact with the client and carrying out all the considerations during the process as an internal dialogue. In many consultation assignments this is fully adequate, but sometimes one needs either to discuss a situation informally with a colleague or to seek formal supervision.

When should the consultant seek supervision? What happens during the supervision—from the supervised person's point of view? What is the potential benefit in relation to carrying out a particular consultation? These are the questions that I address based on my own experience with receiving supervision during consultations.

Supervision is a psychological activity that is traditionally defined as follows:

> Supervision is a contractual, temporary, supportive, catalytic process of professional monitoring, defined in time, where a more experienced person helps a less experienced colleague to integrate professional skills and attitudes so that the colleague becomes better equipped at handling the theories and methods of her profession. [Keiser & Lund, 1991]

Supervision is a helping profession related to consultation. One of the differences between consultation and supervision is the position of "the theories and methods of the profession". In consultation, the professional knowledge is irrelevant to the client-system—as long as it works—whereas the relation between assignment and professional knowledge is essential to the consultant.

Supervision usually takes place as strictly planned activities within the same organization—a counselling centre, a treatment institution, and so forth. The definition mentioned above is more relevant in this sort of context, because the aspect of observation will be more apparent in this situation than in situations where one independent consultant receives supervision from another. The aspect of observation, however, never disappears completely, but it is no more prominent than in other professional contexts, where psychologists have an obligation to be aware of ethical issues and be prepared to intervene and put ethics on the agenda (see section 5.4, "The professional domains").

In a systemic perspective, supervision works because a person (or several persons) step(s) into the picture, working from a *different position* in relation to the assignment than the consultant in charge. In this context, it is the change in position that is important rather than the greater experience. Greater experience—especially with the same type of assignment—is not an advantage in itself, as it may cause the supervisor to simply confirm her colleague's thinking. Greater experience with supervision, however, will be an advantage.

The supervisor should plan the situation with a view to promoting the learning processes of the person who is receiving supervision.

In this context, I will consider supervision *a method for increasing the supervised consultant's irreverence towards her own thoughts and ideas*. Cecchin introduced the concept of "irreverence" (see section 5.3: "From neutrality to irreverence").

When the position changes, it becomes possible to see something else—and to avoid seeing what one saw before. A war memorial in Canberra, Australia, carries the inscription: "And a horizon is nothing more than the limitation of your vision." Regardless how clearly we see the horizon, the horizon is nothing in itself—only the product of our vantage point. The limitation that we choose in a given situation has an influence on the possibilities that we see and the ones we miss.

As consultants, we all have special experiences with people and organizations. We have our prejudices and pet theories. Sometimes, this ballast becomes a prison to the mind rather than a good starting point for progress. It is in situations like these that supervision is an option. But how does a consultant working alone know when such situations arise? I address this issue in the next section, using examples from my own consultations during which I received supervision.

In their fascinating book, Cecchin, Lane, and Ray (1992) mention a number of reasons that a therapist should seek supervision. These reasons are equally valid for the consultant. The consultant may feel that the client is not making any progress, or the client feels stuck and lacks ideas for moving on. The consultant may be held back by too much loyalty to the theories and methods of her firm, or the consultant notices indirect signs via psychosomatic symptoms that something is amiss. When a consultation causes headaches or stomach pains, this may be a sign that the consultant needs help to think along new lines. In that case, supervision is one of the options. In the following section, I describe three incidents, where I benefited from supervision.

Example 1: *When there is a high level of conflict*

I made the decision of seeking supervision at an early stage. Already after the initial request from a new organization, I felt that this was a high-risk assignment with many possibilities of getting caught up in inscrutable psychological games between the various warring parties (Selvini-Palazzoli, 1987). In this situation, I really needed to be watchful and dig in my heels. I therefore contacted a psychologist who works with consultation and supervision from a systemic platform and arranged for continuous supervision adjusted to fit the stages of the consultation. The consultation lasted for three months, and I received supervision five times.

The request was from Brenda, a top manager in a large company in the service sector. She knew me from a management training programme that I had taught. She had been appointed three months earlier and had soon become involved in a conflict between a function manager (Kevin) and many others in a department that had cross-divisional functions for the entire company, which had a total of over 1,000 employees. The department had a poor working environment, a high degree of absenteeism, a high turnover of employees, many complaints from the employees to management and many written complaints from the customers.

My first meeting with management was held in the managing director's office. At the meeting, information was presented that emphasized the complexity of the problem to me. The problem had existed for seven years and had begun after a reorganization, when Kevin had been moved, against his wishes, one step down in the hierarchy. The problem grew, as the head of department and the four function managers—especially Kevin—increasingly expanded the conflict to include other people, both inside and outside the company, in order to find support. Management felt that they had considered and tried "everything". Therefore, they wanted an external consultant to take a closer look at the conditions in the department—and especially at Kevin.

After the first meeting, I was even more pleased with my decision to use supervision. This looked like a tough situation: this organization that had lived with the problem for seven years! I wondered what the various parties would lose if the problem went away? Here was a management team that contained the problem to a *department*. I wondered if it would not be more useful for them to focus on the relationship between management and the department.

The contract came to include individual interviews with the members of the management team, the head of the department and the four function managers, a number of seminars with management separately, the head of department, and function managers together, and all three levels together. Along the way it became necessary to include additional consultations with management. As it turned out, the consultation consisted primarily in assistance to the management concerning its managerial tasks in relation to the department. The assignment was concluded with a mutually binding action-plan that the participants worked out.

Each instance of supervision took its point of departure in my considerations about the stage to come: design and ground rules, angles of attack, and the phrasing of questions for the individual interviews and the preparation of each of the seminars. The supervision was especially helpful for handling the following dilemmas:

1. How to respect demands for confidentiality in the individual interviews, without having to hold back too much useful information? The solution to this was a number of positive reframings at the organizational level.

2. How to vary the consultant's role over time between the extremes: the supportive and optimistic consultant, working in close cooperation, and the confronting and pessimistic consultant, working from a greater distance? Considerations about timing became essential. For example, this comment from my supervisor made me aware that it was time to increase the distance: "It seems that they now trust you so much that they are leaning against you. Be careful not to become a part of the organization—and, thus, a part of the problem. You risk them wanting you to be their in-house psychologist for life. They're going to love you, and nothing is going to change one bit."

3. How to listen respectfully to the contents, without giving up my meta-position in relation to the organizational level? Here, I found help for developing new ways to see events as communication between levels in the organization.

Example 2: *When neutrality is jeopardized*

In this example, I received supervision from colleagues in an informal group for the exchange of experience. We happened to have a meeting at the time when a particular assignment was troubling me. I asked for permission to discuss "a small problem". The case was a follows:

A request had come from a psychologist who was working as a multidisciplinary consultant. He asked for consultation for a group comprising a manager and 10 employees. Most of the employees were dissatisfied with their jobs, the turnover of employees was high, and the lack of faith in the manager was a general issue.

After a meeting with the psychologist and the manager, we made a contract that included three consultations, each lasting one day, with a couple of weeks in between.

The first consultation went well—as the staff and I saw it. But when the manager gave his final evaluation, after the staff members' evaluation, he stated very strongly that he did not see any point in the whole thing at all, nor did he see any chance of improvement.

Three days later, I received a phone call from him. He was very confused and frightened, but did not wish to discuss his management problems. Instead, he repeatedly requested my expert opinion on each of the employees. I refused his request, as it fell outside the scope of the contract. The conversation was unpleasant, partly because it would not end, partly because it was difficult to find a common wavelength.

At this time, supervision became an option. I wanted supervision because of my strong emotions and concerns as to whether I would be able to establish my neutrality strongly enough for me to be able to relate as openly to the manager as I did to the staff.

I was angry with the manager. I felt that I had been manipulated into a one-hour-long telephone conversation that was not included in the contract. I felt sorry for the staff and deeply felt that he was essentially an incompetent manager and a human being in disharmony. These feelings were so strong that I found myself thinking about the assignment constantly, without seeming to get anywhere.

In my opening statement for the supervision, I expressed my problem as one of neutrality and of whether I would be able to find a way for establishing a viable contact with the manager. The supervision, which lasted a little over an hour, consisted of two rounds with the reflections of three colleagues. It led to my personal conclusion that I would break off the group consultation—a decision that I had never before had to make in the middle of a consultation. Instead, I would offer the manager individual consultation. In my following conversation with him he told me that he had gone into therapy. I advised against two parallel processes, but left the offer of individual consultation open for when he was done with his therapy.

The supervision had made the dilemma clear to me: on the one hand, I found it impossible to carry out a consultation for a group when the manager was not willing to consider his own relation to the group. And, on the other hand, I could not bear to end the consultation, out of consideration for the staff, towards whom I felt very protective. This either/or dilemma was resolved when I discovered a third way.

Example 3: *When there is too little doubt*

This was a consultation that included a team of two consultants. We benefited greatly from sparring with each other concerning our thoughts about the organization, the consultation, and potential approaches. After the first request, our first meeting with the institution, and the processing of the findings from the questionnaire survey, I had the opportunity to present the assignment in a group of which I was a member, and which was in the middle of a training programme on systemic consultation.

In this case, my first reaction was to be puzzled at meeting an organization that was so different from my previous experiences. Both my colleague and I had a very clear picture of the organization, which I was now able to present.

The request came from the head of a treatment institution with 35 employees. The institution was used to using consultants each year or every second year. And now it was that time again. Our first meeting was with the head and four members of staff. They asked us for help to work with management, cooperation between the departments, and the institution's options in dealing with increasing demands from the outside world. The consultation was to include one more meeting, a questionnaire survey asking the staff members about suggested themes and what results they would like to see, a two-day seminar, and a follow-up after six months.

We formed the impression that this was an organization with a high level of competence in dealing with various methods within the domain of reflection (see section 5.4). Upon studying more closely the several stacks of papers that we had received on previous development activities, we had the impression of dealing with themes and problem areas on which the organization appeared to have been working for years.

The supervision was based on my fears that this institution wanted us as consultants to simply do "more of the same" (various reflection methods), with the result that everything would stay the way it was. We felt that, in order to enable learning and change, we had to find ways of demonstrating how the institution could convert its insight from the domain of reflection into decisions and actions in the domain of production. We spent many hours talking, trying to develop an understanding of this one organization and its special characteristics.

The supervision led to an acknowledgement that our thorough preparations had made us fall so much in love with our understanding of the organization that we had lost our curiosity to learn about the organization. Where we saw an organization closed to change, we had neglected the risk that we might be closed to signals and input that did not match this understanding.

I also became aware that the theme "It is always the same themes—they just want more of the same" may have been created by our mutual consensus—a consensus that confirmed our good cooperation as consultants. In other words: the challenge before us was to let in the doubt and become better at exploiting our differences as consultants and to place ourselves in a learning position.

This was a very useful insight, which we reached in time for our meeting with the whole staff. We turned it into practice by choosing two very different positions in relation to the organization and carrying out open reflections from these positions. The insight also helped us to change our attitude about the organization and be more humble and hypothesizing. We did not change the planned programme much, but we changed ourselves and the way we realized the programme.

Receiving supervision
and the individual learning spiral

I now discuss these three examples in relation to the individual learning spiral described in chapter 2.

Example 1 (*when the conflict level is high*) dealt with help for going through the learning spiral during each intermittent period. Each time, the supervision began with an initial clarification of the areas where I most needed help. After that, the discourse followed this basic model:

- What had I done since last time? (Stage 1: Concrete experiences of one's own and other people's actions.)

- How did I analyse these events? What had proceeded as expected? What had surprised me? Which events were particularly important to focus on? What had been the most puzzling? (Stage 2: Reflections.)

- How did I interpret these events? What concepts were applicable? What different models of explanation could be formed? (Stage 3: The formation of abstract concepts and alternative hypotheses.)

- What would my focus be in the ensuing intervention? How could I turn my working hypotheses into concrete interventions? (Stage 4: Active experimentation.)

It was different every time at what point in the learning spiral the block and fixation were most pronounced. Questions about my experiences could lead to a different priority of events and attributed meanings (Stage 2). Or ideas for specific actions might be rejected, because the formation of alternative hypotheses turned out to have been neglected (Stage 3). When this became evident, entirely different ideas could occur. The result might be relief stemming from discovering additional options or from feeling more secure about the chosen interventions (Stage 4).

In Example 2 (*when neutrality is jeopardized*), the supervision occurred at an advanced stage in the consultation. The block lay between Stage 1 and 2, where strong emotions were blocking for reflections. Only when I had had an opportunity to get my experiences off my chest and examine them in relation to my values and ideas about professional consultation was I able to move on in the spiral.

In Example 3 (*when there is too little doubt*), the supervision was also received in the middle of a consultation. In this case, our problem, as consultants, was that we were so pleased with and convinced of the products of our own reflections that our formations of alternative hypotheses did not take us far enough (Stage 3). This supervision process can also be seen as a help for us to move from first-order cybernetics, where we were trying to understand the organization, to second-order cybernetics, where we were seeing ourselves as part of the observing system (see section 5.1). The supervision helped us to realize that our enjoyment of our mutual accordance made it easier for us to notice similarities within the organization. In other words, our partnership as consultants had prevented us from noticing differences in the organization over time.

CHAPTER EIGHT

Epilogue

Gitte Haslebo & Kit Sanne Nielsen

In this epilogue, we would like to focus on some issues that are clearer to us now, after working on this book.

Consultation work requires personal development

Working as an organizational consultant is a complicated affair. And sometimes we ask ourselves: What is our motivation for this line of work? Why do we find it interesting, exciting, educational and enriching—and at other times difficult, hard, draining, and stressful?

What personal characteristics do we need in order to work in the sometimes chaotic and complex situations that we find ourselves in? What is a good position to take when working as an organizational consultant? In reflecting on these questions, we have arrived at the following: We need to be sincerely and openly interested in our surroundings, to use our thinking intuitively and to be willing to take on tasks that, at first glance, appear daunting. We aim for an interaction between equals and respect the ideas, feelings, and experiences of the members of the organization. We are aware that they have done the best they could in a given situation. We should therefore be open and understanding towards those people who are positive towards our entrance into the organization as well as the ones who are more reserved or negative towards us.

By asking the agents in the client-system, "Who are you?" "What would you like to be?" "How can you achieve that?", we are confronted with those same questions ourselves. When studying psychology—specifically developmental psychology— we learned that identity is developed through a biological and psychological process of maturation with occurring built-in conflict phases stretching from birth to death. In systemic thinking, identity is seen primarily as the product of interpersonal interaction. Identity is linked to the relations that involve the individual in particular situations, periods, or contexts. Consultation offers many challenges to work with one's own identity in relation to one's role as consultant.

This means that we have to be curious about ourselves, work on our own possibilities and limitations, and constantly challenge our own identity as professionals.

We believe that *we, as consultants, need to set off the time and energy to work with our own personal development*. This is a prerequisite for us to learn both how best to function as consultants and how to create a productive relationship with our clients. Every time, this cooperation has to be created from scratch—based on respect for this particular client's unique history, self-knowledge, and visions for the future.

Systemic thinking and method contain elements that, in our opinion, have been capable of renewing our cognition processes and our understandings of complex organizational issues. We have found it a fascinating working method. By understanding individual systems and seeing them in other contexts and by understanding our own position in different contexts, we are able to move around and assume different positions. We may, for example, listen and empathize, control and confront, or wonder and reflect. This variation of possibilities has provided us with the necessary space to develop as consultants.

Consultation work
is a learning process in itself

When we work as consultants, it is important that we stay in the field of tension between knowing and not knowing. When we take on a new assignment, naturally we meet the new client-system with our knowledge of theory and method, our experiences with organizations in this and other areas, and our basic knowledge about this particular organization. The challenge is to be able to employ this knowledge from a position of *not knowing*. We have to learn about the organization and from its members. We have to learn while we carry out the assignment. We learn from the interactions and the relations that we have with the members of the organization. We exchange points of view and understandings, and in this process we also become more conscious of and critical of the knowledge and assumptions with which we met the organization. Examining the possibilities and limitations created by human thinking becomes a joint project. We let others observe us, and we get their reactions and their assessment of our efforts. This gives us new knowledge about what we do and how others perceive the quality of what we do. Our most important task may be to listen behind the words and add new approaches. This way, we ourselves find new approaches, based on our own experiences. Systemic thinking is an approach, an understanding of meaning, that allows us to test various hypotheses and interventions based on the notion that there is no absolute truth or *one* right way to accomplish an assignment. We need to decide on the next step, take it, and see what happens—and *allow ourselves to use the ensuing events as feedback and as a chance to learn.*

The end of the information society?

In our part of the world, the societal self-image has long been that we live in the information society. Information technology has enabled us to access and process large amounts of knowledge and information—and, increasingly, make them accessible to lay persons. This is true of organizations too. Not only can individual working procedures be controlled more efficiently through information technology—the daily working situation of the individual manager or employee has become loaded with knowledge and information as well. Management information systems, e-mail, and so forth place a growing demand on the individual to stay up-to-date on general aspects of the company's situation and development. Internet access is going to increase the demands for staying up-to-date on global events of relevance to the company, its product development, corporate strategy, marketing, and so forth. The large amounts of information that each employee has to take in and process on a daily basis require constant learning and the development of new skills on the job. Information technology has helped us cope with a tremendous complexity of detail. But are we any wiser from it? This is, increasingly, the pressing question. Our enthusiasm for the information society has been dampened by our realization that huge amounts of information do not necessarily lead to wisdom and insight.

Something is missing. We believe that *meaning* is the missing link. Information in itself does not make managers and employees more efficient or creative. New information is just as likely to cause confusion and a sense of insecurity, anxiety, anger and frustration. Sometimes these reactions are labelled "resistance to change". Another way of understanding these reactions is to see them as a lack of understanding of the big picture or of the meaning of the organizational process that has been caused by a particular change—what it means to the organization, to the colleagues, and to *me*. Knowledge that we cannot relate to ourselves is "dead" knowledge. We can learn dead knowledge by rote (for example, next year's budget, the corporate strategy, the human resources policy), but we cannot transform it into action until we are able to link it to our job, our role, our skills, our relations with other people in the organization, our identity, values, and plans for the future. These links are what create meaning.

We believe that we are about to leave the self-image implied by the term the "information society" and on the way to a new one that has not found a name yet.

Future leaders have to be experts
at learning processes

The coming phase is going to require new skills. It is not so much
the ability to gather and process large amounts of information that
is going to be important, but, rather, the ability to *ignore* information—or, put more positively: the ability to focus or to go to the
heart of the matter. The question: how can I find out *more*? is going
to be replaced by the question: how can I find out what it is *necessary or useful* to know? The selection procedure is going to be of
the essence.

This is going to lead to a new question: What criteria should
we use for selecting? This inevitably points to the ethical dimension. In order to be able to discriminate, we have to be conscious
of the values that guide us. This issue has become apparent in
recent years in a number of research areas (how much more do we
want to know about efficient pesticides? about biological warfare?
about the survival rates of premature babies?). No research area
lies outside the ethical dimension, and neither do the daily search
for information or the acquisition of knowledge in the organization. The ability to select is going to become increasingly important to avoid being overwhelmed and stunned by the information
load. Without this ability, the tremendous information load is going to pose more of an obstacle than a tool for progress. The challenge is to be able to select the relevant aspects that provide
meaning and usefulness in the given context.

Only when we know what is essential can we make decisions
and act. The path to a deeper understanding of the organization
that one is a member of or consult to, therefore, also leads in-
wards. How do we know that we know? How do we come to
know what it is important to know? These questions direct attention towards one's own process of cognition. This introspective
approach cannot, however, stand alone. We have to test what we
think we know in a dialogue with others. The dialogue is what
provides the inspiration for putting our intuitive and non-verbal
knowledge and experiences into words. This exchange between
introspection and expression is an important part of the meaning-
forming process.

* * *

It is our belief that it is going to be an increasingly important management task to contribute to the development of these new skills. Management may do this by making the time and space available for managers and staff to work with the selection and assessment of information, individual and shared values, cognition processes, and dialogue involving everybody in the organization. In this sense, the challenge to managers will be to act as *experts at learning processes.*

REFERENCES AND BIBLIOGRAPHY

Amtoft, M., & Strøier, V. (1996). Brug af metaforer i organisationsudvikling. *Fokus på Familien*, 2: 101.

Andersen, S. B., Betting, K., & Haslebo, G. (1970). *Proceskonsultation. Organisationsudvikling.* København: Dansk Psykolognyt, Nr. 17.

Andersen, T. (1990). *The Reflecting Team.* New York: W.W. Norton.

Anderson, H., Goolishian, H., & Winderman, L. (1986). Problem-determined systems: towards transformation in family therapy. *Journal of Strategic and Systemic Therapies*, 5: 1–14.

Argyris, C. (1985). *Strategy, Change and Defensive Routines.* London: Pitman.

Argyris, C. (1991). Teaching smart people how to learn. *Harvard Business Review* (May–June).

Argyris, C. (1993). *Knowledge for Action. A Guide to Overcoming Barriers to Organizational Change.* San Francisco, CA: Jossey-Bass Inc.

Argyris, C., & Schön, D. A. (1978). *Organizational Learning: A Theory-in-Action Perspective.* Reading, MA: Addison-Wesley.

Bateson, G. (1972). *Steps to an Ecology of Mind.* New York: Ballantine Books.

Bateson, G. (1979). *Mind and Nature: A Necessary Unity.* New York: Bantam.

177

178   REFERENCES AND BIBLIOGRAPHY

Bennis, W. G., Benne, K. D., & Chin, R. (1969). *The Planning of Change* (second edition). New York: Holt, Rinehart and Winston.

Bévort, F., Jensen, P. E., & Prahl, A. (Red.) (1995). *Engagement i arbejdet. Involvering i organisationer.* Århus: Handelshøjskolens Forlag.

Bion, W. R. (1961). *Experiences in Groups and other Papers.* London: Tavistock Publications.

Block, P. (1981). *Flawless Consultation. A Guide to Getting Your Expertise Used.* Texas: Austin.

Bor, R., & Miller, R. (1991). *Internal Consultations in Health Care Settings.* London: Karnac Books.

Borwick, I. (1986). The family therapist as business consultant. In: L. C. Wynne, S. H. McDaniel, & T. T. Weber (Eds.), *Systems Consultation. A New Perspective for Family Therapy* (pp. 423–440). New York/ London: Guilford Press.

Boscolo, L., & Bertrando, P. (1993). *The Times of Time. A New Perspective in Systemic Therapy and Consultation.* New York/London: W.W. Norton.

Bridges, W. (1992). *The Character of Organizations. Using Jungian Type in Organizational Development.* Palo Alto, CA: Consulting Psychologists Press.

Campbell, D. (Ed.) (1995). *Learning Consultation. A Systemic Framework.* London: Karnac Books.

Campbell, D., Coldicott, T., & Kinsella, K. (1994). *Systemic Work with Organizations. A New Model for Managers and Change Agents.* London: Karnac Books.

Campbell, D., Draper, R., & Huffington, C. (1991a). *A Systemic Approach to Consultation.* London: Karnac Books.

Campbell, D., Draper, R., & Huffington, C. (1991b). *Second Thoughts on the Theory and Practice of the Milan Approach to Family Therapy.* London: Karnac Books.

Cecchin, G. (1987). Hypothesizing, circularity, and neutrality revisited: an invitation to curiosity. *Family Process, 26:* 405–441.

Cecchin, G., Lane, G., & Ray, W. A. (1992). *Irreverence. A Strategy for Therapists' Survival.* London: Karnac Books.

Cecchin, G., & Stratton, P. (1991). Extending systemic consultations from families to management. *Human Systems, 2:* 3–13.

Cooperrider, D. L. (1990). Positive image, positive action: the affirmative basis of organizing. In: S. Srivasta, D. Cooperrider, et al., *Appreciative Management and Leadership.* San Francisco: Jossey-Bass Publishers.

Cronen, V., & Lang, P. (1994). Language and action: Wittgenstein and

Dewey in the practice of therapy and consultation. *Human Systems*, 5 (1–2).

Cronen, V., & Pearce, W. B. (1980). *Communication, Action and Meaning: The Creation of Social Realities*. New York: Praeger.

Dell, P. (1986). Why do we still call them "paradoxes"? *Family Process*, 25: 223–234.

de Shazer, S. (1985). *Keys to Solutions in Brief Therapy*. New York: Norton.

de Shazer, S. (1988). *Clues. Investigating Solutions in Brief Therapy*. New York: Norton.

Dewey, J. (1934). *Art as Experience*. New York: G.P. Putnam: Capricorn Books.

Dickson, A. (1982). *A Woman in Your Own Right?* London: Quartet Books.

Dixon, N. (1994). *The Organizational Learning Cycle: How We Can Learn Collectively*. London: McGraw-Hill.

Dougherty, M. A. (1990). *Consultation. Practice and Perspectives*. Pacific Grove, CA: Brooks/Cole Publishing.

Engman, K., & Söderqvist, M. (1992). "Det var inget fel på oss". Om lösningsfokuserad personalgrupp. *Fokus på Familien, 3:* 168–177.

Friedman, E. H. (1986). *Emotional Process in the Marketplace*. In: L. C. Wynne, S. H. McDaniel, & T. T. Weber (Eds), *Systems Consultation. A New Perspective for Family Therapy* (pp. 398–422). New York/ London: Guilford Press.

Fruggeri, L., Telfner, U., Castellucci, A., Marzari, M., & Matteini, M. (1991). *New Systemic Ideas from the Italian Mental Health Movement*. London: Karnac Books.

Gergen, K. J. (1985). Social constructionist theory: context and implications. In: K. J. Gergen & K. Davis (Eds.), *The Social Construction of the Person*. New York: Springer Verlag.

Handy, C. (1986). *Understanding Organizations*. Harmondsworth: Penguin.

Haslebo, G. (1973). Betingelser for indlæring om magt og konflikt i forskellige undervisningssystemer. In: G. Haslebo et al. (Eds.), *Magt og påvirkning i systemer*. København: Reitzels Forlag.

Haslebo, G. (1995). Livsorientering og organisationskultur. In: Jørn Laursen (Ed.), *Karriere og livsforløb*. København: Danmarks Forvaltningshøjskoles Forlag.

Haslebo, G., Holbøll, P., Høyrup, S., Madsen, F. H., & Nejsum, B. (Eds.) (1973). *Magt og påvirkning i systemer. Nogle socialpsykologers overvejelser omkring ændring af sociale systemer*. København: Hans Reitzel.

180   REFERENCES AND BIBLIOGRAPHY

Hirschhorn, L. (1995). *The Workplace Within.* London: MIT Press.

Hoffman, L. (1985). Beyond power and control: toward a "second order" family systems therapy. *Family Systems Medicine, 3* (4): 381–396.

Holme, M., & Humle, A. S. (1991). *Fra problem til løsning. Samtalebehandling på systemisk grundlag.* København: Akademisk Forlag.

Høyrup, S. (1975). *Laboratorie- og sensitivitetstræning.* Anvendelsen af intensiv gruppetræning til social indlæring og -udvikling. København: Gyldendals Pædagogiske Bibliotek.

Huffington, C. (1996). *Own notes from a personal interview.* London: Tavistock Institute.

Huffington, C., & Brunning, H. (Eds.) (1994). *Internal Consultancy in the Public Sector. Case Studies.* London: Karnac Books.

Jensen, P. (1994). *Ansikt til ansikt. System- og familieperspektivet som grunnlag for klinisk sykepleie.* Norge: Ad Notam Gyldendal.

Johnsrud Langslet, G. (1996). Løft av organisasjoner. Løsningsfokusert tilnærming til utvikling og problemløsning. *Fokus på Familien 2*: 84.

Keiser, L., & Lund, M. A. (1991). *Supervision og konsultation.* København: Socialpædagogisk Bibliotek.

Kolb, D. A. (1984). *Experiential Learning. Experience as the Source of Learning and Development.* Englewood Cliffs, NJ: Prentice-Hall.

Kuhn, T. S. (1962). *The Structure of Scientific Revolutions.* Chicago: University of Chicago Press.

Laing, R. D. (1961). *The Self and Others.* London: Tavistock.

Lang, P., Little, M., & Cronen, V. (1990). The systemic professional domains of action and the question of neutrality. *Human Systems, 1* (1).

Lewin, K. (1951). *Field Theory in Social Sciences.* New York: Harper & Row.

Lingås, L. G. (1993). *Etik for social- og sundhedsarbejdere. En grundbog.* København: Hans Reitzels Forlag.

Maturana, H. R., & Varela, F. J. (1980). *Autopoiesis and Cognition: The Realization of the Living.* Dordrecht: Reidel.

Maturana, H. R., & Varela, F. J. (1987). *The Tree of Knowledge: The Biological Roots of Understanding.* Boston: New Science Library.

McCaughan, N., & Palmer, B. (1994). *Systems Thinking for Harassed Managers.* London: Karnac Books.

Morgan, G. (1986). *Images of Organization.* London: Sage.

Morgan, G. (1993). *Imaginization: The Art of Creative Management.* London: Sage.

Myers, I. B. with Myers, P. B. (1993). *Gifts Differing.* Palo Alto, CA: Consulting Psychologists Press.

Pearn, M., Roderick, C., & Mulrooney, C. (1995). *Learning Organizations in Practice*. London: McGraw-Hill.

Penn, P. (1982). Circular questioning. *Family Process, 21* (3): 267–280.

Piaget, J. (1971). *Psychology and Epistemology*. Harmondsworth, Middlesex: Penguin Books.

Poulfelt, F. (1982). *Konsulentlære*. København: Nyt Nordisk Forlag.

Poulfelt, F. & Brask, J. (1989). *Ledelsen og konsulenten—om brug af konsulenter*. København: Nyt Nordisk Forlag.

Raelin, J. A. (1985). *The Clash of Cultures: Managers and Professionals*. Boston: Harvard Business School Press.

Rice, C. A., & Scott Rutan, J. (1987). *Inpatient Group Psychotherapy: A Psychodynamic Perspective*. London: Macmillan.

Risling, A. (1989). *Konsult i organisation*. Stockholm: Natur Och Kultur.

Schein, E. H. (1985). *Organizational Culture and Leadership*. San Francisco, CA: Jossey-Bass.

Schein, E. H. (1987). *Process Consultation. Volume II. Lessons for Managers and Consultants*. Reading, MA: Addison-Wesley.

Schein, E. H. (1988). *Organizational Psychology*. Englewood Cliffs, NJ: Prentice-Hall.

Schjødt, B., & Egeland, T. A. (1991). *Fra Systemteori til Familieterapi*. Oslo: Tono.

Schön, D. A. (1983). *The Reflective Practitioner. How Professionals Think in Action*. New York: Basic Books.

Selvini-Palazzoli, M. (1987). *The Hidden Games of Organizations*. New York: Pantheon Books.

Selvini-Palazzoli, M., Boscolo, L., Cecchin, G., & Prata, G. (1978). *Paradox and Counterparadox*. New York: Jason Aronson.

Selvini-Palazzoli, M., Boscolo, L., Cecchin, G., & Prata, G. (1980). Hypothesizing–circularity–neutrality: three guidelines for the conductor of the session. *Family Process, 19* (1): 3–12.

Senge, P. M. (1990). *The Fifth Discipline. The Art & Practice of The Learning Organization*. London: Century Business.

Swieringa, J., & Wierdsma, A. (1992). *Becoming a Learning Organization. Beyond the Learning Curve.* Wokingham, UK: Addison-Wesley.

Thyssen, O. (1994). *Kommunikation, kultur og etik*. København: Handelshøjskolens Forlag.

Tomm, K. (1984). One perspective on the Milan systemic approach: Part I. Overview of development; theory and practice. *Journal of Marital and Family Therapy, 10*: 113–125.

Tomm, K. (1985). Circular interviewing: a multifaceted clinical tool. In: D. Campbell, & R. Draper (Eds.), *Applications of the Milan Approach to Family Therapy*. London: Grune & Stratton.

Tomm, K. (1987a). Interventive interviewing, Part I: Strategizing as a fourth guideline for the therapist. *Family Process, 26*: 3–13.

Tomm, K. (1987b). Interventive interviewing, Part II: Reflective questioning as a means to enable self-healing. *Family Process, 26*: 167–183.

Tomm, K. (1988). Interventive interviewing, Part III: Intending to ask lineal, circular, strategic, or reflective questions? *Family Process, 27*: 1–15.

von Foerster, H. (1979). *Cybernetics of Cybernetics*. New York: Gordon & Breach Science.

von Foerster, H. (1981). *Observing Systems*. Seaside, CA: Intersystems Publications.

von Glasersfeld, E. (1984). An introduction to radical constructivism. In: P. Watzlawick (Ed.), *The Invented Reality*. New York: W.W. Norton.

Watzlawick, P. (Ed.) (1984). *The Invented Reality*. New York: W.W. Norton.

Watzlawick, P., Beavin, J., & Jackson, D. D. (1967). *The Pragmatics of Human Communication*. London: W.W. Norton.

Wiener, N. (1961). *Cybernetics* (2nd ed.). Cambridge, MA: M.I.T. Press.

Wilkes, J., & Wilkens, M. (1993). Training for systemic management. *Human Systems, 4*: 331–347.

Wynne, L. C., McDaniel, S. H., & Weber, T. T. (Eds.) (1986). *Systems Consultation. A New Perspective for Family Therapy*. New York/London: The Guilford Press.

Zenger, J. H., Musselwhite, E., Hurson, K., & Perrin, C. (1994). *Leading Teams. Mastering the New Role*. San Jose, CA: Zenger-Miller.

INDEX

183

placebo effect, 131
"Positive Image—Positive Actions"
    (Cooperrider), 131
positive reframing, 127–128, 130–
    133
positive thinking, 131–133
practice, use of systemic thinking,
    95–99
Prata, G., 102, 110, 111
prehension, 18–19
private meaning structures, and
    collective learning, 35–36
problem(s):
    and makeup of participant
        group, 29–31
    and meaning, 2–3
    and the observer, 5–8
    relations in consultation, 10
    as resources, 61
    solving, in organizational
        consultation, 17–38
production, domain of, 117–119,
    120, 122
project description [case study],
    76–77, 79–80
punctuation, 104–105
Pygmalion experiment, 131–132

Raelin, J.A., 118
Ray, W. A., 113, 144, 151, 163
re-telling, hypothesis, 123
reality, different versions of, 95–
    96
referral, 33
reflection, 135–137
    domain of, 119–122
    room for, 98
reframing, 127–128
    case study, 58
    see also positive reframing
relations, impact on events, 96–97
respect, and curiosity, 112
responsibility:
    and actions, 28

case study, 46
Rice, C. A., 134, 155
ritual, directions for, 133–134
Roderick, C., 17
role expectations, and directions
    for action, 133–134

Scott Rutan, J., 134
segmented consultation, 38
Selvini-Palazzoli, M., 102, 110, 111,
    163
seminars [case studies], 56–59, 83–
    88, 91–92
Senge, P. M., 97
size, of participant group, 30
Stratton, P., 126
subject area, defining, 12–15
subjectivity, 119–120. See also
    cybernetics
supervision, 1, 153, 161–170
    case study, 44, 52, 59
Swieringa, J., 21, 26
symptoms, 7
system, defining, 8–10
"Systemic Professional Domains
    of Action and the Question
    of Neutrality" (Lang et al.),
    115
systemic thinking, 1, 68, 71
    cybernetics, 98–99, 101–103
    domains, 115–122
    hypothesizing, 123–128
    interventions, 128–138
    linear and circular thinking, 104–
        110
    neutrality and irreverence, 110–
        115
    use in practice, 95–99

Tavistock Institute, 140–141
team spirit, and management [case
    study], 52, 66–67
theme days [case studies], 43, 47–
    53, 61, 62–63